W9-BTH-565

JEHOVAH'S WITNESSES

BY
SALEM KIRBAN

DOCTRINES OF DEVILS
No. 3

Exposing the cults of our day

MOODY PRESS
CHICAGO

Library of Congress Catalog Card No. 75-124142
MOODY PRESS EDITION, 1973
ISBN: 0-8024-4291-9

ACKNOWLEDGMENTS

To Dr. Gary G. Cohen, Professor of Greek and New Testament at Biblical School of Theology, Hatfield, Pennsylvania, who carefully checked the final manuscript and supplied the scripture references.

To Bob Krauss, artist, who skillfully did the finished art throughout the book.

Printed in the United States of America

Cathedrals or Converts

Charles Taze Russell believed in the welfare and good health of his followers. Perhaps he had heard the familiar advice:

Eat breakfast like a king
Eat lunch like a prince
but
Eat dinner like a pauper.

My wife, Mary, and I arrived at Bethel, World Headquarters of Jehovah's Witnesses in Brooklyn, New York at "prince" time. And the brothers and sisters (that's how they refer to each other)...all 1500 of them...had just finished consuming 1200 pounds of chicken.

Actually, we arrived just after the lunch period...just in time to see the "brothers" take away the dishes and stack them in the dishwasher. At Bethel, it's the "brothers" who do the dishes. Each brother gets three weeks of Dish Duty. The "sisters" have other responsibilities...among which include working in the slaughterhouse on one of the three farms outside of Brooklyn.

We didn't stay for supper but the sister who took us on our guided tour assured us that no meat is ever served at suppertime—another Charles Taze Russell idea. Eating meat at night, he remarked, keeps one awake and causes dreams.

Who is Charles Taze Russell? He is the founder of the cult today known as Jehovah's Witnesses.

While, unfortunately his theology is not Bible based...(and therefore, Christians should turn away from such teaching)...some of his other ideas could give us some true food for thought.

Sound eating habits, good nutrition...all go to make for a more efficient Christian witness. And what's even more important, have you ever known a Jehovah's Witness congregation to build a cathedral?

Have you ever seen a Jehovah's Witness congregation exceed a local membership of 200 members? Most likely not. For when it does exceed this number...it is subdivided and a new church is built in a new location.

And what type of church structure is built? A cathedral? A $75,000 or $150,000 structure? Absolutely not. Have you ever seen the little inexpensive Kingdom Halls that Jehovah's Witnesses have?

Why?

Because they believe more in the message. To them the message...their message...is more important than the building.

This is where the Christian church has made a great mistake. We have been putting our money into buildings instead of the message. It is the message that is the POWER—"...the gospel...is the power of God unto salvation..." (Romans 1:16).

And so Jehovah's Witnesses, in one 15 year period (1941-1956) tripled their membership...because they believe in converts...not cathedrals!

AFTERTHOUGHTS IN ALLEGHENY

Since its founding in 1879, the Jehovah's Witnesses have only had three Presidents.

Charles Taze Russell (lived 1852-1916) was the first President. He was born in a little nondescript town then called Allegheny...now a part of Pittsburgh. Joseph L. and Anna Eliza Russell, his parents, were Presbyterians of Scotch-Irish descent.

Joseph L. Russell was quite an industrious man...building up a chain of clothing stores that one day would net his son more than a quarter of a million dollars! In fact Charles Russell, at the age of fifteen, was already in partnership with his father!

While brought up in a Presbyterian background, by 15 he had joined the Congregational church. The more he attended church, however, the more he claimed that organized religion "...merely wrecked my confidence in human creeds and systems of Bible misinterpretations."[1]

During the next few months Russell reflected over the subject of religion and was in a quandry as to which direction to turn. Then he relates:

> Seemingly, by accident, one evening I dropped into a dusty, dingy hall in Allegheny, Pa., where I had heard religious services were held, to see if the handful who met there had

---

[1]E. T. Clark, *The Small Sects in America*, Rev. Ed. (1949), pp. 33,34.

> anything more sensible to offer than the creeds of the great churches. There, for the first time, I heard something of the views of Second Adventism, by Jonas Wendell....[2]

It was then that Charles Taze Russell, at 18, along with a few friends, formed a class for Bible study which continued from 1870 to 1875. Russell, however, was disappointed by the Adventist view that Christ was coming back again in the flesh. He was convinced that His Second Coming would be a spiritual or invisible one. Thus Russell soon had afterthoughts about meeting in the dingy hall in Allegheny. His newly organized Bible class of six members, which included his father, nevertheless, became the first nucleus group of Jehovah's Witnesses.

In light of this, Russell issued his first pamphlet. It was titled *The Object and Manner of the Lord's Return.* He published 50,000 copies and this began what is now perhaps the largest publishing venture in the world!

His afterthoughts in Allegheny mushroomed into one of the largest cults in the world. Perhaps no other religious movement has each state, each country, each city, each block, and each street...as thoroughly graphed out as has the Jehovah's Witnesses!

By his own admission Russell borrowed from the Adventists such doctrines as the extinction of the soul at death, the annihilation of the wicked, the denial of hell and then over the years, he proceeded to add his own pet theologies...which orthodox Christians believe to be in direct contradiction to God's Word.

PARTNERS IN PHILADELPHIA

"...Russell's study group had come to realize that when Christ returned it would not be in the flesh, as commonly believed...when Jesus should come he would be as invisible as though an angel had come."[3]

Russell was on a business trip to Philadelphia and came across a publication by N. H. Barbour of Rochester, N.Y. entitled, *The Herald of the Morning.* In reading this publication he was enthusiastically surprised to learn that Barbour held the same views as he on the invisible return of Christ. He was particularly interested in the chronology set forth in the magazine.

Chronology is the science of arranging time in periods and ascertaining the dates and historical order of events. Russell's entry

[2] *Watch Tower Reprints*, p. 3821.

[3] *Jehovah's Witnesses in the Divine Purpose*, Watch Tower Bible & Tract Society, (1959), p. 18.

into this field would later prove embarrassing to the Jehovah's Witness cult when he set dates for the Second Coming of Christ.

Russell urged Barbour to meet with him...and paid his expenses for the trip. Barbour was a printer and Russell had money. Between the two of them (the Pittsburgh group and the Rochester group), they now together published the magazine *The Herald of the Morning.*

It was then that Russell curtailed his clothing business activities...and when finally liquidated, this brought him more than a quarter of a million dollars!

Russell was determined, in his own misguided way unfortunately, that he would shun material wealth and "test the Lord's approval" of his ministry. He set down for himself four criteria for his future work. He would:

(1) Devote his life to the cause
(2) Invest his fortune in the promulgation of the work
(3) Prohibit collections at all meetings
(4) Depend on unsolicited contributions (wholly voluntary) to continue the work after his fortune was exhausted[4]

At the time he set forth these principles he was only 25 years old. In 1877 Russell and Barbour published a 194-page book titled, *Three Worlds or Plan of Redemption.*

> This book set forth their belief that Christ's second presence began invisibly in the fall of 1874 and thereby commenced a forty-year harvest period. Then, remarkably accurately, they set forth the year 1914 as the end of the Gentile times....[5]

Thus, as early as 1877 Charles Taze Russell, the founder of Jehovah's Witnesses, went on record specifying that Christ had invisibly returned in 1874!

Finally, in a disagreement on theology, Russell and Barbour parted ways and a new chapter in Russell's life was to begin.

A NEW MAGAZINE AND MARRIAGE

The year 1879 was a memorable year for Charles Taze Russell. This was the year he founded the new publication, *Zion's Watch Tower and Herald of Christ's Presence.* On July 1st he printed 6000

[4]*Studies in the Scriptures,* 1918 Ed. Vol. 7, Watch Tower Bible & Tract Society (1917), p. 55.
[5]*Qualified to be Ministers,* Watch Tower Bible & Tract Society (1955), p. 300.

This display in the printing plant of Watchtower headquarters indicates the vast worldwide circulation of Jehovah's Witnesses publications.

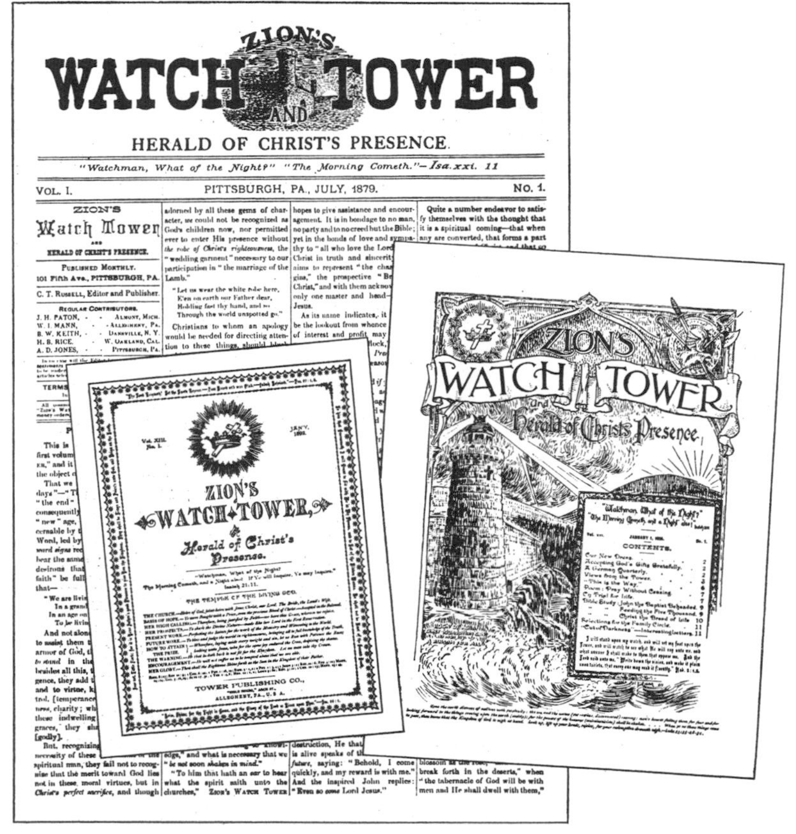

ZION'S WATCH AND TOWER

HERALD OF CHRIST'S PRESENCE.

"Watchman, What of the Night?" "The Morning Cometh."—Isa. xxi. 11

VOL. I. PITTSBURGH, PA., JULY, 1879. NO. 1.

ZION'S Watch Tower and HERALD OF CHRIST'S PRESENCE.

PUBLISHED MONTHLY.
101 Fifth Ave., PITTSBURGH, PA.

C. T. RUSSELL, Editor and Publisher.

REGULAR CONTRIBUTORS.
J. H. PATON, - - ALMONT, MICH.
W. I. MANN, - - ALLEGHENY, PA.
B. W. KEITH, - - DANSVILLE, N. Y.
H. B. RICE, - - W. OAKLAND, CAL.
A. D. JONES, - - PITTSBURGH, PA.

adorned by all these gems of character, we could not be recognized as God's children now, nor permitted ever to enter His presence without *the robe of Christ's righteousness*, the "wedding garment" necessary to our participation in "the marriage of the Lamb."

"Let us wear the white robe here,
E'en on earth our Father dear,
Holding fast thy hand, and so
Through the world unspotted go."

Christians to whom an apology would be needed for directing attention to these things, should blush

hopes to give assistance and encouragement. It is in bondage to no man, no party and to no creed but the Bible; yet in the bonds of love and sympathy to "all who love the Lord ... Christ in truth and sincerity ... aims to represent "the cha... gins," the prospective "B... Christ," and with them ackno... only one master and head— Jesus.

As its name indicates, it ... be the lookout from whence ... of interest and profit may

Quite a number endeavor to satisfy themselves with the thought that it is a spiritual coming—that when any are converted, that forms a part

...

But, recognizing ... necessity of these ... spiritual man, they fail not to recognize that the merit toward God lies not in these moral virtues, but in *Christ's perfect sacrifice*, and though

edge," and what is necessary that we "*be not soon shaken in mind.*"

"To him that hath an ear to hear what the spirit saith unto the churches," ZION'S WATCH TOWER

destruction, He that ... is alive speaks of th... *future*, saying: "Behold, I come quickly, and my reward is with me." And the inspired John replies: "Even so come Lord Jesus."

blossom as the rose, ... break forth in the deserts," when "the tabernacle of God will be with men and He shall dwell with them,"

Vol. XIII. No. 1. JAN'Y. 1892.

ZION'S WATCH TOWER, and Herald of Christ's Presence.

"Watchman, What of the Night?
The Morning Cometh, and a Night also." ... Isaiah 21:11.

THE TEMPLE OF THE LIVING GOD.

TOWER PUBLISHING CO., ALLEGHENY, PA., U. S. A.

ZION'S WATCH TOWER and Herald of Christ's Presence.

"Watchman, What of the Night?"
"The Morning Cometh, and a Night also!" Isaiah

CONTENTS.

"I will stand upon my watch, and will set my foot upon the Tower, and will watch to see what He will say unto me, and what answer I shall make to them that oppose me. And the Lord said unto me, 'Write down the vision, and make it plain upon tablets, that every one may read it fluently.'" Hab. 2:1, 2.

July, 1879 issue of WATCH TOWER. Left inset, January, 1892. Right inset, January 1, 1895.

copies. Today that publication is known as, *The Watchtower Announcing Jehovah's Kingdom.* It has grown from 6000 copies *monthly* to many millions *weekly*! In fact, every *week* throughout the year the Brooklyn printing plant publishes more than *four million* magazines that keeps 14 of their 30 high-speed presses busy all the time!

In the magazine's second issue under the heading "Do You Want 'Zion's Watch Tower'?" it said:

> "Zion's Watch Tower" has, we believe, JEHOVAH for its backer, and while this is the case it will never *beg* nor *petition* men for support. When He who says: "All the gold and silver of the mountains are mine," fails to provide necessary funds, we will understand it to be time to suspend the publication.[6]

Two years later the name and identity of Jehovah were discussed. In the issue of July 1882 a 7 page article appeared entitled "Hear, O Israel! Jehovah Our God Is One—Jehovah." This article sought to disprove the doctrine of the Trinity—which teaches of one God in three persons.

Perhaps this was the key article that set up Charles Taze Russell as one who believed that he was appointed to serve as the witness of Jehovah. *Jehovah's Witnesses in the Divine Purpose* on page 22 makes the following statement:

> ...of all the early voices heard, Jehovah had chosen the publication we now call *The Watchtower* to be used as a channel through which to bring to the world of mankind a revelation of the divine will and, through the words revealed in its columns, to begin a division of the world's population into those who would do the divine will and those who would not...This little group, headed by C. T. Russell had now been tested and had been found fit to undertake the great preliminary campaign leading up to the climax expected in 1914...

With this challenge in mind, Russell's followers were urged to forsake *"Christendom's apostate religion and learn the truth, then actively spread that truth to others."*[7]

Charles Taze Russell then married Maria F. Ackley in Pittsburgh. She had become interested in him through his teaching. She answered many of the letters and also wrote articles for *Zion's Watch Tower.* They had no children.

---

[6]*Watch Tower*, August 1879, p. 2.

[7]*Jehovah's Witnesses in the Divine Purpose*, p. 23.

For a while Mrs. Russell served as the first secretary-treasurer of the society as well as associate editor. However, 18 years after their marriage, in 1897, Mrs. Russell separated from her husband. And in 1913 she sued Charles Taze Russell for divorce on the grounds of "his conceit, egotism, domination, and improper conduct in relation to other women."[8] What Mrs. Russell meant as far as "improper conduct" has never been made clear. It may have been her way of threatening for a large cash settlement...for when confronted in court she admitted that she did *not* mean to imply that her husband was guilty of adultery. The divorce suit was settled with a payment of $6,036 to Mrs. Russell.

The divorce settlement did reveal that Charles Taze Russell activities in the religious field were carried on through several subsidiary societies and that all the wealth that flowed into him through these societies was under the control of a holding company. Russell held $990 of the $1000 capital of the holding company and two of his followers the other $10.

FULL SPEED AHEAD...THE CHURCH PICKETS

Charles Taze Russell's new magazine, *Zion's Watch Tower*, proved to be an important part of the expansion movement of Jehovah's Witnesses. By 1880 some 30 congregations had come into existence from Pennsylvania to Michigan.

On December 13, 1884 this Society was granted a legal charter and was organized as a corporation (From 1881 to 1884, it had been established as an unincorporated body).

Thus the official chartered beginning of the Jehovah's Witness movement was in 1884. It was at this point that Russell issued a 7-volume series of doctrinal books. The first volume appeared in 1886 and was called *The Divine Plan of the Ages*. The entire series was first called *Millennial Dawn*. It later became known as *Studies in the Scriptures*. The books enjoyed an astoundingly wide circulation...over 6 million copies of the first volume were distributed over a 40 year period.

The first headquarters of the Watch Tower Society was in Allegheny, Pennsylvania. But by 1889 they had outgrown this and built their own structure. This "Bible House" served for 20 years. The name had now changed from "Zion's Watch Tower Tract Society" to "Watch Tower Bible and Tract Society of Pennsylvania."

---

[8]Herbert H. Stroup, *The Jehovah's Witnesses*, Columbia University Press (1945), pp. 9-11.

Russell made his first trip abroad in 1891 and by 1900 the society had established a branch office in London...then Germany in 1903, and another one in Australia in 1904. Jehovah's Witnesses were expanding!

In 1894 two industrious ladies selling the *Watch Tower* entered into a lawyer's office in New York. The lawyer seeing the two young ladies, and seeking not to be impolite, bought three of their booklets.

That lawyer turned out to be Joseph Franklin Rutherford...who later became a Russell convert, then the Society's lawyer, and finally the Society's second President!

Charles Taze Russell was not one to let any grass grow under his feet. Determined to make a dent in the denominational churches...Russell called for volunteers from his Society to engage in a church-picketing service. The plan...to distribute his booklets to people as they left their churches on Sunday. He leaned heavily on Jeremiah 7:2 for this plan.

The April 15, 1899 issue of *Zion's Watch Tower* outlined some of the tactics:

> The...plan of operations is for the friends who will so engage in each city or village to lay out a program which will insure that no congregation be omitted and that none be served twice.
>
> All large congregations require at least two or three for proper rapid service as they come out.
>
> And generally the effect is better if the distributors locate half a block away from the church building in each direction in which the people go.

The plan was worked for many years and eventually it led to house-to-house distribution of tracts on Sunday mornings.

Needless to say...the hostile reaction to this invasion was intense. To further their cause even more, the Watch Tower society went one step farther.

> To assist them (the Christians) in their resignation (from their local church) and to provide a further testimony to those in the church systems responsible for removing their names from the church rolls, specially printed "Withdrawal Letters" were provided, beginning in 1900.

Thus the Jehovah's Witnesses moved full speed ahead from church picketing to the printing of Withdrawal Letters. And with their growth... opposition began.

TO HELL AND BACK

The subject of Hell was one of Charles Taze Russell's favorite topics. From 1905 to 1907 Russell delivered his lecture "To Hell and Back" throughout the entire United States and Canada.

Jehovah's Witnesses do not believe in Hell as a place of torment. They only believe that Hell is a common grave of mankind where *everyone* dying goes until time for the resurrection.

On March 10, 1903 a ministerial alliance proposed a debate with Russell. They chose Dr. E. L. Eaton, minister of the North Avenue Methodist-Episcopal Church. The six-day open debate was to begin on Sunday, October 18, 1903, and the site of the confrontation was Pittsburgh, Pennsylvania.

> Eaton debated affirmatively that the Bible teaches that divine grace for salvation has been exercised since man's fall...that there will be no probation after death.
>
> Russell denied this Bible truth.
>
> Eaton affirmed that the soul does not die nor is unconscious after death.
>
> Russell denied this.
>
> Eaton affirmed that the Bible teaches that all the saved will enter Heaven.
>
> Russell denied this.
>
> Eaton affirmed that the Second Coming of Christ is for Christians only.
>
> Russell denied this.
>
> Eaton affirmed that the Bible teaches that Hell is the divine penalty for all who reject Christ.
>
> Russell vigorously denied this hell-fire doctrine.

The above debate, and Russell's denials, is reported in the Watch Tower's own book, *Jehovah's Witnesses in the Divine Purpose*, pages 41-42.

Russell and his following believed that they had won the debates...especially the last one on Hell. So convincing was Russell that even some of Dr. Eaton's own congregation became Jehovah's Witnesses. One attending clergyman, acknowledging a victory for Russell, was reported to have told him, "I am glad to see you turn the hose on hell and put out the fire."[9]

It may be fair to say that had Russell given his lecture, "To Hell and Back" to a group of clergymen today...his converts would

---

[9]J. F. Rutherford, *A Great Battle in the Ecclesiastical Heavens* (1915), p. 10.

have surpassed the few he convinced in 1903. With the growth of liberal churches and apostasy running rampant...Russell would have had a field day with many of today's churches and their congregations...who are "Ever learning, and never able to come to the knowledge of the truth" (2 Timothy 3:7).

To the millions of Jehovah's Witnesses who have followed Charles Taze Russell...he did succeed in turning the hose on hell and putting the fire out.

Nevertheless, the Word of God stands true and hell as a literal place of torment will be their destiny unless they come to a saving knowledge of Christ.

It is sad to report that Jehovah's Witness relished the stand of Charles Taze Russell's lecture "To Hell and Back," and they reported as follows on page 43 of *Jehovah's Witnesses in the Divine Purpose:*

> In this striking lecture he took his audience on a witty, humorous, imaginary trip to hell and back. The irrefutable arguments presented by Russell in this talk, and by the Bible Students themselves throughout the entire period, made a lasting effect on many people.

THE PHANTOM SPEAKER and MIRACLE WHEAT

Accompanying his success, attacks on Charles Taze Russell began to mount from within his own ranks. In the *Watch Tower* of 1909, page 371 Russell commented:

> From various quarters the word came to us that the leaders of classes were protesting that WATCH TOWER publications should not be referred to in the meetings but merely the Bible.
>
> This sounded loyal to God's Word; but it was not so. It was merely the effort of those teachers to come between the people of God and the *Divinely provided light upon God's Word.* Let us remember that Satan is behind such a move as that!

With the growing movement Russell sent his legal counselor, J. F. Rutherford to New York to secure new headquarters. They bought the old four-story brownstone parsonage of Henry Ward Beecher at 124 Columbia Heights in Brooklyn. This address is now the world headquarters of Jehovah's Witnesses.

Russell began an intensive campaign of witnessing, first with tracts and then with an international newspaper syndicate of his sermons sent out to some 3000 newspapers.

From December, 1911 to March, 1912 Russell with 7 men went on a worldwide tour. He reported back on sermons he delivered in Hawaii and other tropical islands.

A Jehovah's Witnesses worker preparing orders for shipment overseas. Note old fashioned record player in foreground...no longer used.

The *Brooklyn Daily Eagle* through private investigation on its part proved that in Hawaii Russell never delivered a sermon and that his "searching investigations" into the missions of China and Japan was in effect simply spending a few hours in each country. The *Brooklyn Daily Eagle* published these findings on page 18 in the February 19, 1912 issue.

To some Russell became known as the "phantom speaker." Apparently his advance agents became overzealous in selling this world tour both as to the countries visited and in their reports back to the United States.

The *Brooklyn Daily Eagle* continued for a while in having a heyday in exposing the advertising scheme behind the "tour." However, in spite of this adverse publicity, Jehovah's Witnesses continue to grow.

By this time the Watch Tower circulation had risen to 55,000. Russell now also hired convention trains for special speaking engagements throughout North America and Europe.

Russell was accused of many fraudulent schemes. The "Miracle Wheat" episode of 1913 probably was the most famous.

Russell's periodical once advertised this so-called "Miracle Wheat" for $1 a pound. He claimed it would grow five times as fast as any other type. The *Brooklyn Daily Eagle* had doubts. They published a cartoon ridiculing the "Miracle Wheat" and Russell. Russell sued the newspaper for $100,000 for libel.

Government officials investigated the wheat. They found it not to be five times as good, but slightly inferior to ordinary wheat.

The *Brooklyn Daily Eagle* won the suit! The announcement of the decision of the court was published on page 16 of the January 29, 1913 issue of The *Brooklyn Daily Eagle.*

The Phantom Speaker...the Miracle Wheat...and now the Greek scholar. When Rev. J. J. Ross, pastor of the James Street Baptist Church of Hamilton, Ontario sought to expose Russell in a pamphlet...Russell sued him.

In court Russell lied and claimed he knew Greek. When confronted with the Greek alphabet, he was unable to read it. Russell, who had asked his public to believe that he had gone back to the Scriptures in their original language, Greek and Hebrew, to give the world the correct interpretation of essential passages...had to admit he had lied and could not read Greek!

DRAMA and DEATH

In 1914 Russell climaxed the fulfillment of a dream...that of producing a film presentation with the synchronization of sound on records. It was called "The Photo-Drama of Creation." It cost the Society $300,000. It was a clever presentation of Russell's theology and misrepresented orthodox churches comparing their theology as worse than that of heathen idols.

By 1916 Charles Taze Russell's health was failing fast. In the fall of that year, though extremely sick, he left New York for a lecture tour which would take him to California. On this trip, he delivered his last public address in San Antonio on October 24th.

Arriving in California in weakened condition he decided to return to his Brooklyn headquarters.

He died enroute on October 31, 1916 on an eastbound train at Pampa, Texas. Wrapped in a "toga" (made at his own request), Russell passed away.

Charles Taze Russell served Jehovah's Witnesses for 32 years. It is said that "...he traveled more than a million miles as a public lecturer, preached more than 30,000 sermons and wrote books totaling over 50,000 pages, often dictated a thousand letters a month, and managed every department of a world-wide evangelistic campaign employing some 700 speakers."[10]

Yet Jehovah's Witnesses have never published a biography of their Founder!

HERE COMES THE JUDGE

How could one man like Charles Taze Russell, with little formal education, achieve such great success? His training in theology was shallow and yet he commanded huge audiences...even held them spellbound.

No doubt his policy of "Free—No Collection" attracted many. (It reminds us of the Armstrong cult which stresses in THE PLAIN TRUTH magazine that "...you cannot pay for your own subscription....")

And like Herbert W. and Garner Ted Armstrong...Russell had the ability to attract and hold audiences.

In his books he quoted from over 5000 Scriptural references. And while much of his theology was *not* Scriptural...it appeared rational to his listeners. His favorite subject was Hell and he set out to deny the reality of Hell as the eternal destination of unbelievers. This

[10]*Studies in the Scriptures*, Vol 7, Watch Tower Bible & Tract Society, p. 57.

subject endeared many to Russell who wished to get rid of eternal punishment.

But perhaps his greatest method (and one many Christians have not yet fully appreciated even today) was his emphasis on literature and books. This contributed immeasurably to the rapid and continued growth of the Jehovah's Witnesses.

Now Russell was gone. And a successor had to be chosen. In those days every $10 contribution to the Society entitled its donor to one voting share. Russell, when alive, could cast 25,000 votes...since he had contributed about $250,000. This gave him the power to quash any unrest. In fact this voting method was not amended by the Watchtower Society until 1944. Now each member only has one vote.

On January 6th, 1917 there were 600 in attendance at the annual meeting of the corporation...with 150,000 votes. Joseph Franklin Rutherford, known by his followers as "Judge" was unanimously elected.

Rutherford was born November 8, 1869 in Booneville, Missouri. His parents were Baptists.

Rutherford's father was a farmer and his income was limited. When his son Joseph at 16 decided to go to college to study law...his father agreed providing that his son earn his own way and *also* pay for a hired hand to take his place on the farm.

The son agreed and paid his way through college by learning shorthand, a skill he continued to practice up to his dying day.

After law school, at 22, he was admitted to the Missouri bar and became a trial lawyer. Later he became a special judge in the 14th Judicial District of Missouri. For 15 years he continued this practice until his sudden acquaintance with the two Watchtower girls who came to his law office to sell him books. This was in 1894.

Both Rutherford and his wife started to study this new-found doctrine. Very little is available on Rutherford's wife. In Edmond Charles Gruss' excellent book, *Apostles of Denial*, he reports receiving a letter from The Watchtower Bible and Tract Society, November 30, 1960 which read:

> Brother Rutherford did have a wife. She was an invalid, however, and lived on the west coast. This may be partly the reason why she is not mentioned in biographical material as Brother Rutherford spent his time generally on the eastern coast in New York City. His wife did believe in the truth although his son did not.

"Judge" Joseph F. Rutherford, the late much heralded President of Jehovah's Witnesses, shown in a 1938 photograph. Rutherford was speaking in front of his colorful ornamental curtain at Leichardt Stadium during a visit to Sydney, Australia.

Russell and Rutherford had two distinct opposing personalities. Russell was most always in the public eye and very popular. Rutherford avoided public appearances as much as possible and avoided photographers.

Russell was kind, tactful and knew how to meet people graciously. Rutherford was more direct and sharp. He seemed quite distant, cold and reserved. But the Judge was here to stay. And he was to reign for 25 years!

THE OPPOSITION...AND THE BOMBSHELL

To oppose Rutherford was, in his opinion, equivalent to questioning the authority of Jehovah Himself. Soon, some of his followers would find this out.

When Rutherford became President he reorganized the Brooklyn headquarters. He increased the number of field representatives (called Pilgrims) from 69 to 93. Their responsibility was to see that Rutherford's edicts were carried out or as the Watchtower Society puts it, "...to assist the brothers to maintain their optimistic view...."[11]

He increased the activity of local congregations in "pastoral work." Each city was to be divided into territorial districts. "Sisters" were to systematically make calls to loan books and to encourage people to attend the chart talks on the "Divine Plan" which were to be given in that neighborhood.

Rutherford also set up what he called "Ministers of the Word of God." These men were responsible for delivering Studies in the Scriptures.

Rutherford was an imposing figure when attired in his familiar wing collar, bow tie and black suit. Frequently he was seen with his reading glasses hung on a string and this accentuated the impression of dignified importance. He was to write over 100 books and pamphlets and his works were to be translated into over 80 languages.

One of the first books released under Rutherford's administration was to cause a split.

Some, seeing Rutherford's stranglehold of power, sought to have a more democratic governing of their Society through Board action...rather than the action of one man.

Others felt Rutherford was displacing Russell, their founder, and nullifying his importance to the Society.

---

[11]*Jehovah's Witnesses in the Divine Purpose*, p. 66.

One man to question Rutherford's authority was P. S. L. Johnson. At one time a minister of a denominational church...Johnson later "came to the knowledge of the truth" and became a Witness. He served as a Speaker for the Society in Great Britain and was a brilliant man. The Watchtower Society claims "This brilliance finally led to his downfall."[12]

Johnson was recalled to New York, but once there he tried to persuade Rutherford to send him back to England. Rutherford refused. Soon Johnson was able to secure help from four of the seven Board Members. They were in favor of returning Johnson to England. Since the Board of Directors consisted of only seven men, this meant Johnson had won the majority. It also meant that the majority of the Board of Directors were now on this point in direct opposition to President Rutherford.

In the meantime Rutherford authorized the loyal board members to publish the last and 7th volume of Studies in the Scriptures. This was to be a compilation of writings Russell had never completed. It was called, *The Finished Mystery.*

The majority of the board members were unaware of Rutherford's authorization of the compilation of this new book...since they had not been consulted.

Noon, July 17, 1917 was a momentous day. Judge Rutherford gave a present of this book to each member of the Bethel family. Bethel is the name of the Headquarters office.

The new book came as a bombshell! Completely surprised by its release, the opposing members of the Board of Directors (who were in the majority) became engulfed in a 5 hour controversy. In fact, they aired their views to the entire staff.

It became evident that other staff members were sympathetic with the dissident board members...so Judge Rutherford took some fast action.

Rutherford, an astute lawyer, reminded the board members that although Russell had appointed them to fill vacancies...such appointments had not been reconfirmed at the annual meeting at Pittsburgh...hence they were not legal members of the Board.

Rutherford's "rabbit out of the hat" trick, while astute, culminated in a split in the Watchtower Society. The dissident board members spread their opposition throughout the land. As a result, after the summer of 1917, many of the congregations all over the world were composed of two parties.

[12]*Jehovah's Witnesses in the Divine Purpose*, p. 69.

From this split came the Dawn Bible Students (which sponsored the coast to coast radio program, "Frank and Ernest") and the Laymen's Home Missionary Movement.

The Dawn Bible Students believe that revelation ceased shortly before Russell's death. Jehovah's Witnesses stress a progressive revelation which, incidentally, has repudiated many previous doctrines and interpretations of the Scripture set forth by Russell.

THE JUDGE GOES TO JAIL

The Finished Mystery, the book that Rutherford had introduced and which caused the split...was a success. Within 7 months the Society's outside printers had printed 850,000 copies.

Perhaps bolstered by the popularity of this book...the Society decided to publish a 4-page tabloid size extract from *The Finished Mystery.*

It was called "The Fall of Babylon—Why Christendom Must Now Suffer—The Final Outcome."

December 30, 1917 was chosen as the distribution day. It was a Sunday. Jehovah's Witnesses on this day were to begin distributing 10 million copies of this tract.

At the time the nation was embroiled in World War I.

And this tract, in the words of the Watchtower Society:

> ...showed how Catholic and Protestant religious organizations together formed modern-day Babylon, which must soon fall to oblivion. On the back page was a graphic cartoon picturing a rampart or wall crumbling, with stones being thrown down, one by one, that were marked: "Protestantism," "Creeds," "Eternal torment theory," "Doctrine of trinity," "There is no evil," "No pain," "No death," "No devil," "Apostolic succession...."[13]

The furor which this tract aroused soon took the form of governmental action. Canada, tied to England in World War I, banned the Watch Tower Society and imposed a fine of $5000 and five years in prison for anyone in possession of the books which were deemed seditious...and full of anti-war statements.

Judge Rutherford had laid the keel for the Society. He began to build an organization far more absolute and far more rigidly organized than was the Catholic Church which he so bitterly opposed.

Now with opposition mounting, Rutherford was beginning to claim that the Watch Tower Society of Brooklyn would carry millions of

[13]*Jehovah's Witnesses in the Divine Purpose*, p. 74.

people across the fields of Armageddon into the Millennium, in which it would emerge as "The New World Society" to last a thousand years.

Rutherford had convinced his followers that the Tribulation Period had begun in the first half of the month of November, 1914. This began the period of active "witnessing" which was to lead to persecution. And now, 3½ years later, the United States District Court for the Eastern District of New York issued a warrant for the arrest of 8 of the Society's principal officers...which included Judge J. F. Rutherford!

This was May 7, 1918. *Jehovah's Witnesses in the Divine Purpose*, on page 79, states: "On that day the forty-two months or 1,260 days of Revelation 11:2,3 ended...and now three and a half years later it was being killed by Satan's symbolic *wild beast*, as Revelation 11:7 foretold."

It is amazing how so many cults so brazenly twist Scriptures to conform to their own circumstances. In the eyes of the Jehovah's Witnesses the Tribulation Period started November, 1914, and the first 3½ years ended when their Witnesses were arrested.

After a 15 day trial, on June 21st seven of the eight Witnesses were sentenced to 20 years in jail. Judge Rutherford was among them.

With the war over the Witnesses were released, after having served nine months of imprisonment. A decision of the court, made on May 14, 1919, established that Rutherford and his associates had been imprisoned on an illegal conviction.

In fact, later Rutherford was to practice law before the Supreme Court of the United States.

During his stay in jail Rutherford contracted a lung condition. It remained with him the rest of his life.

But he returned to the Presidency of the Watchtower Society as a martyr-hero and this imprisonment served only to cause him to make even more bitter the attacks on government and organized religion.

The Society was on the move. And on October 1, 1919 they published a new voice, THE GOLDEN AGE.

With this publication the Society purchased their own printing press which they fondly called, "The Old Battleship."

The Old Battleship was to print millions of copies of *The Golden Age* and also *The Watch Tower.*

The Judge had been to jail...but this experience jettisoned him and the entire Witness movement to new heights of grandeur.

NEW LIGHT FOR A NEW AGE

Fresh from his victory Judge Rutherford began to see "new light" and slowly Russell's writings, person and books were forgotten.

Rutherford believed in progressive revelation. To Rutherford this meant that God had a definite time to reveal certain Bible facts. And Rutherford was that chosen vessel and the Watch Tower organization became God's sole dispenser of truth. Each of Rutherford's new books was, in effect, a fresh revelation of new truth which God had imparted to him. A previous emphasis on Bible study was now being replaced with more stress on the placing of literature, the making of calls and the faithful reporting of these calls to Watchtower Headquarters.

Literature distribution became a keystone. The first year the Society purchased their own press in 1920, 38 carloads of paper were used in producing more than 4 million copies of *The Golden Age.* And by 1922 larger printing quarters were needed!

Rutherford's flood of new books brought increased dissension. He, however, wisely used Russell's own writing to attempt to put out the brush fires. In the July 15, 1906 issue of the *Watch Tower* Russell commented:

> Some who have The Three Worlds or the *old* edition of Day Dawn would perhaps like to know my present opinion of them—whether I still think them profitable books to loan to truth-seekers. To this I reply, Certainly not; because the very immature views of God's truth therein presented fall far short of what we now see to be God's wonderful plan....

And this further bolstered Rutherford's theory of progressive revelation.

Friday, September 8, 1922 was designated by the Witnesses as "The Day." That day was the mid-point of an 8 day international convention at Cedar Point, Ohio. 18,000 were in attendance.

It was here that Judge Rutherford composed a stinging resolution which included:

> ...all efforts of the denominational church organizations, their clergy, their leaders and their allies, to save and reestablish the order of things in the earth and to bring peace and prosperity must of necessity fail, because they do not constitute any part of the kingdom of the Messiah...

Then followed further paragraphs "exposing the disloyalty of the

4 THE BIBLE STUDENTS MONTHLY, Brooklyn, N. Y. Vol. 9, No. 9

THE FALL OF BABYLON

(Continued from Page 3, Column 4.)

writer of Sunday School lessons, in commenting on the lesson for September 2nd, 1917, ... mutual destruction. God pity the clergy for what is coming upon them ...

hateful bird.—Babylon has contained both the best and the worst, but the worst have predominated.

18:3. For all nations have drunk of the wine of the wrath of her fornication.—The wine of false doctrine is that of the Divine right of kings, divine right of the clergy and eternal ...

represents the masses of the people and especially the restless discontented class. And thus shall great Babylon perish from the earth and her name shall be forgotten forever!!

UNIVERSAL PEACE WITH REJOICING.

... will pervade ...

Illustration shows the Fall of Babylon as portrayed by Jehovah's Witnesses in The Finished Mystery. Drawing shows falling blocks depicting the Trinity, immortality of the soul, eternal torment, etc. as false doctrines.

Floor upon floor of printing presses constantly grind out Jehovah's Witnesses publications. At this press, pictured above, the paper starts out in a roll and moves at rapid speed with the press printing both sides at one time...quickly emerging at a completely trimmed and bound Watchtower magazine. The blurred sheet in the photo indicates the fast speed of this printing press.

clergy for their participation in World War I."

Judge Rutherford, in front of that large audience, was in his glory as he urged his "brothers and sisters" to go:

> ...back to the field, O ye sons of the most high God! Gird on your armor! Be sober, be vigilant, be active, be brave. Be faithful and true witnesses for the Lord. Go forward in the fight until every vestige of Babylon lies desolate. Herald the message far and wide. The world must know that Jehovah is God and that Jesus Christ is King of kings and Lord of lords. This is the day of all days. Behold, the King reigns!
>
> You are his publicity agents. Therefore, advertise, advertise, advertise, the King and his kingdom.[14]

And advertise they did. Some 35 million copies of his resolution condemning the church were printed and distributed.

The die had been cast. The stirring cry of Judge Rutherford to "...advertise, advertise, advertise..." was the base of a continuing campaign to publish and print books, booklets and magazines in order to build the sinews of their world organization. In the frame reference of Exodus 11:2,3...the denominational Christians were the "Egyptians." All the while the profit from these book sales were in turn building up the Watchtower empire.

This was a new age...and Judge Rutherford, as "spokesman for Jehovah" had brought a new light!

UPPER AND LOWER CLASSES

Rutherford was writing so many books because of his "new revelations" that the presses could not keep up with him. A 1936 issue of the *Watch Tower* reported:

> Too many and too rapid now are those unfoldings of Bible prophecy and truths, so that books cannot be written and published fast enough by the Watch Tower Society to present them all. But YOU CAN GET THEM in the only magazine of its kind: The Watchtower.

Rutherford saw himself as Elisha, anointed in the place of Elijah (Russell) to carry on the work. And carry on he did!

In 1920 with "The Old Battleship" printing press the Society averaged 1000 booklets a day. By 1921, this rose to 3000 per day. By 1923 it was 6000 per day, by 1926 it zoomed to over 10,000 per day. Today they have the capacity to produce 50,000 *bound* books a day!

Rutherford became interested in establishing a new "mode of

[14]*Watch Tower*, 1922, pp. 333-335.

worship." Brothers were encouraged to get out their word...sell books for their Kingdom Service. Their spirituality was measured in terms of time quotas, book placement quotas and attendance quotas. It was important that they strive to meet their quotas. Major emphasis shifted even more from study to service and servicing the neighborhood within their allotted quota.

In fact, on June 12, 1927 a young man wrote Rutherford about this very thing:

> Instead of having a public meeting it was thought well to have a *one hour* canvassing drive.
>
> Right after the morning talk, 35 of the friends engaged in field work, with the result that 240 books were sold...

The letter was signed by N. H. Knorr...who was later to become the third President of the Society in 1942.

This became the pattern...selling books became the emphasis. And the "Egyptians" were the very ones who would buy these books to support their rapidly growing cult.

Rutherford proceeded to set up a heavenly class of followers separated into two divisions:

Mordecai-Naomi Class (begun about 1918)

This was the remnant of the 144,000 on earth with which Christ made up the Watch Tower body of Christ.

However, according to Witness reports, a large number of this class became unfaithful and became part of the "evil slave class."

Therefore the

Ruth-Esther Class (from 1922 to 1929)

came into existence to fill the vacancies left by the defectors.

Jonadeb Class (1931)

This class was known also as the "Great Multitude." They did not seek after the spirit-begotten or "born again" experience.

Later on Rutherford had another "revelation" and the Jonadeb Class, then referred to as the "Great Company" or the "Great Multitude" was relegated to an earthly unregenerate class.

The *Mordecai-Naomi Class* had been told that they were the last members of the organized Body of Christ on earth. Only this 144,000 were to rule with Christ in the heavenly sphere. For this they quote Revelation 7:4 and 14:1,3 but neglect to notice that the 144,000 are all of the 12 tribes of Israel, hence Jewish.

Those who didn't make that class filtered down into the *Ruth-Esther Class.*

Finally, came the Jonadebs..."the hewers of wood and the carriers of water." They adapted this from the slave relationship of the Gibeonites to Joshua and the Israelites (Joshua 10:10-27). For them the door of Heaven, according to Witness doctrine, is shut...they are not spirit-begotten.

With the chaos and confusion of so many classes...it was time for Rutherford to come up with a new revelation. This time he simplified it.

There were two classes...

THE HEAVENLY CLASS

This was the 144,000

By 1931 this Class was all filled up...all 144,000...Rutherford announced. But the overflow crowd was not to despair. There was to be another class...

THE EARTHLY CLASS

Today, the majority of Jehovah's Witnesses belong to this "Earthly Class."

Since the door to Heaven was shut in 1931 by Judge Rutherford...all present Jehovah's Witnesses will never get to Heaven! That is why Jehovah's Witnesses of today tell you they do not desire to go to Heaven. Their hope is to live here forever on earth. And since Heaven is not their home...*they do not need to be born again!* (Actually there are some 9000 living Jehovah's Witnesses who still claim to be part of the 144,000).

THE PENNY REWARD

To set the pace for future programs of literature distribution the Watch Tower Society used the parable of the Penny (Matthew 20:1-16).

They explained that this parable described the work done by the Watch Tower Society since 1919 and up to 1931. The Watch Tower Society was the "vineyard of God." The 12 years from 1919 to 1931 were the 12 hours of the parable. This work day had come to an end. Now the "Faithful and Wise Steward" to whom all these goods had been given was now about to pay out the Penny.

That reward was announced in July, 1931 at a convention in Columbus, Ohio attended by some 15,000 followers.

The reward: Their new name was to be JEHOVAH'S WITNESSES! This was their Penny!

Why the new name? One reason is given in *Jehovah Witnesses in the Divine Purpose*, page 125:

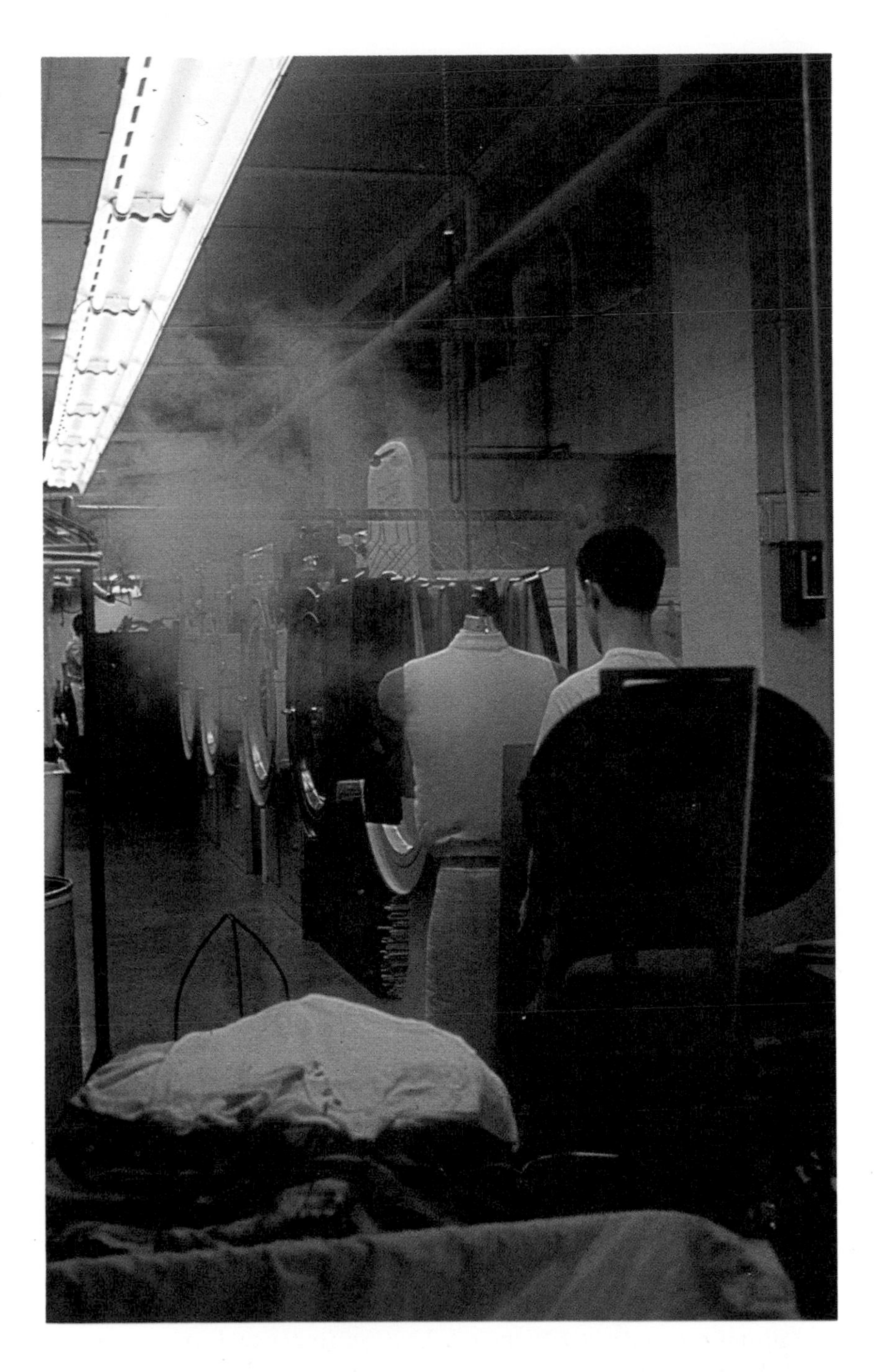

The laundry at Watchtower headquarters in Brooklyn where the "brothers" press some 150 shirts an hour, 6000 a week...all for a salary of $14 a month!

...outsiders generally called us "Millennial Dawn people" and reproachful names, such as "Russellites."

The New World Society had been formed; a theocracy (a Government headed by God) had been established.

The designation of "Jehovah's Witnesses"...has become the emblem of a New World society.[15]

Rutherford, by the name change, had finally virtually disassociated himself from the Founder, Russell, and by so doing, undoubtedly misled many trusting souls into believing that his and Russells' were two different organizations.

In fact a personal letter from the Society to Walter R. Martin, February 9, 1951 revealed:

We are not "Russellites" for we are not following Charles T. Russell or any other imperfect man. Honest examination of our literature today would quickly reveal that it differs widely from that of Russell's, even though he was the first President of our Society.

The Class structure had been set...the "quota" book salesmen were off to a running start...and the bright shiny new Penny in the form of a new name...JEHOVAH'S WITNESSES had successfully embarked.

THE CASE OF THE MISSING PRINCES

Charles Taze Russell was a date setter. And it often got him into hot water...as well as his successor, Rutherford.

But Rutherford could always lean on progressive revelation and claim a "new revelation."

Russell taught that the "ancient worthies" or "princes" would be resurrected" after the Gospel Church has been glorified..."[16] He referred to Abraham, Isaac, and Jacob, etc.

The time of the resurrection of these princes was given as 1914 by Russell.[17] When 1914 came and went and nothing occurred...a new revelation was necessary.

Rutherford, writing in 1920, changed the date of the return of the princes to 1925:

...Scriptures definitely fix the fact that there will be a resurrection of Abraham, Isaac, Jacob and other faithful ones of old, and that these will have the first favor. We may expect 1925 to witness the return of these faithful men of Israel...[18]

---

[15]*New Heavens and New Earth*, p. 235. To arrive at a new name, they based their selection on Isaiah 43:10-12; 62:2 and Revelation 2:17.

[16]*Studies in the Scriptures*, III, p. 265.

[17]*Studies in the Scriptures*, III, p. 94.

[18]*Millions Now Living Will Never Die!*, p. 88.

Again, the princes did not arrive on earth. And therefore it was necessary for a new "revelation" to come to the "channel."

Rutherford wrote in 1928 that:

> ...it may be reasonably concluded that the "ancient worthies" will be back on earth as perfect men within a comparatively short time.[19]

Finally, in 1929, perhaps to raise his sagging hope, Rutherford had "Beth Sharim" (House of Princes) built in San Diego. This was built to provide a place for the princes to stay when they returned.

It appeared that a primary aim of the Watch Tower Society was to increase greatly the sale of their books. Each year Rutherford came out with at least one new book. To increase zeal among the brethren, the Judge offered many of the faithful two books free for every one book they sold.

Two years before his death Rutherford claimed that over 300 MILLION copies of his writings had been circulated.

On January 8, 1942, Rutherford died. He was 72 and had served as President of the Watch Tower Bible and Tract Society (Jehovah's Witnesses) for 25 years.

He had united the loose congregations into a "Theocratic" dictatorship. "Beth-Sharim," Rutherford's home for the coming "princes" was sold shortly after his death.

The Princes never arrived!

A THIRD LEADER ARISES

It was Nathan H. Knorr who wrote Judge Rutherford in 1927 of how successful he was in selling Watch Tower books on Sunday.

Knorr had come a long way since then.

Nathan Homer Knorr was born in Bethlehem, Pennsylvania in 1905. He graduated from Allentown, Pennsylvania High School in June, 1923. When 16, he resigned from membership in the Reformed Church and associated himself with the Allentown congregation of Jehovah's Witnesses.

At 18 he became a full-time preacher and joined the headquarters staff at Bethel in Brooklyn. By 1932 he became general manager of the publishing office and plant. By 1934 he was elected as one of the directors of the Society's New York corporation...and in 1940 he was made a director and chosen as vice-president of the Pennsylvania corporation, Watch Tower Bible and Tract Society.

On January 13, 1942 he was elected to become the third President

[19]*Millions Now Living Will Never Die!*, p. 88.

of the Watch Tower Society.

Although not well known he had demonstrated his ability quietly as an organizer and a leader. He was an accomplished writer and speaker.

With Knorr came a vigorous program of expansion with emphasis on education. In 1942, when Knorr took over there were about 115,000 Witnesses. Today there are over 1½ Million!

In 1943 Knorr established the Gilead Watchtower Bible School near Ithaca, New York. Gilead was moved to the Brooklyn headquarters in 1961. Here a 10 month crash-training course was instituted.

By 1957 it was necessary to build a new 13-story printing plant...and a 10-story addition in 1967, but the publishing demands still grew.

Jehovah's Witnesses came out with their own version of the Bible...*The New World Translation*...in 1961. It reflected their doctrinal views. Under Knorr's leadership...all writings are now anonymous. There are no more leading personalities. Terminology has changed.

Local assemblies were termed "companies."
    They are now called "congregations."

Workers were called "Publishers."
    They are now called "ministers."

Meetings used to be in homes and rented halls.
    They are now in Kingdom Halls.

Emphasis on sales has now been coupled with emphasis on scholarship. The Witness door to door approach is now prepared and tactful.

With Knorr's regime...there has been a tremendous expansion of the work into foreign countries. In 1942 witnessing was carried on in 54 countries. Today Witnesses are active in over 200 countries!

The most publicized parts of Knorr's program are the Yankee Stadium conventions in New York City. In 1950 they attracted some 123,000 followers; in 1953 over 165,000, and by the time the 1958 assembly met both at Yankee Stadium and the Polo Grounds...over ¼ million attended.

The International Assembly of Jehovah's Witnesses of 1969 was held in the United States and Europe from July 6 to August 17th. Over 840,000 people attended these Assembly meetings.

And with a new leader and more to come...Jehovah's Witnesses continue to grow.

Watchtower Society's international headquarters at 124 and 107 Columbia Heights in Brooklyn, New York. This is "Bethel," home of the Watchtower Bible School of Gilead and administration offices for worldwide movement.

BLOOD TRANSFUSIONS BANNED

A faithful member of the Jehovah's Witnesses will not accept a blood transfusion...nor will he allow a blood transfusion to be given to any member of his family. They believe the giving or the taking of blood transfusions is a violation of God's covenant of the sanctity of life.

> Jehovah's witnesses do not reject blood for their children due to any lack of parental love...They know that if they violate God's law on blood and the child dies in the process, they have endangered that child's opportunity for everlasting life in God's new world.[21]

They also believe

> It may result in the immediate and very temporary prolongation of life, but that at the cost of eternal life for a dedicated Christian. Then again, it may bring sudden death, and that forever.[22]

When a 5-year-old was brought to the Massachusetts General Hospital suffering from a serious congenital heart defect in 1970, there was little question that open-heart surgery could make the child well. The parents refused to approve the operation because it required blood transfusions.

The boy was chronically short of breath and exhausted, and chances that he would survive to adulthood were slim. The doctors were stymied. Transfusions were essential to this heart operation.

The doctors considered going to court to obtain temporary custody of the boy, so that they could operate without the parent's consent. The parents warned that if such action were taken, they would refuse to admit their son back into their home.

About 7 months later the doctors came up with a solution. They would drain 2½ pints of blood from the child into three plastic bags that would remain connected to a blood vessel in the boy's left arm during the operation.

Since the blood had technically never left the child's body, it could be returned to his blood stream after surgery without being considered a transfusion in the religious sense. To replace the blood during surgery, doctors administered 6 pints of a mild salt solution called Ringer's lactate.

When the surgeons had repaired the child's heart, the blood in the plastic bags flowed back into the boy's body...the lactate solution was then excreted normally.

Through this unusual dilemma, the doctors had come up with a

[21]*Blood, Medicine and the Law of God*, p. 54.
[22]*Blood, Medicine and the Law of God*, p. 55.

COMPARATIVE CHARTS on the RESURRECTIONS and JUDGMENTS

THE BIBLE vs. JEHOVAH'S WITNESSES

Published by SALEM KIRBAN Inc., Kent Road, Huntingdon Valley, Penna. 19006.

Library of Congress Catalog Card No. 75-124142

Resurrection	Group "Resurrected"	How Resurrected into *new creations*[1]	Time of Resurrection
The First Resurrection	Christ and the 144,000 (The Annointed Class)	Spiritual. Invisible to the human eye. Raised with spirit bodies.	1918
The Second Resurrection	*The Resurrection of Life* includes: **1.** Old Testament people who were faithful to God **2.** Faithful men to God who lived at the time of Christ but died before Pentecost **3.** The Other Sheep (Jehovah's Witnesses who are not part of the 144,000 and who died before Armageddon). *(Paradise Lost,* pp. 228, 229; *You May Survive Armageddon,* p. 355)	Raised with physical bodies[2]	The Millennium (". . . ea after Armageddon . . ." *You May Survive Armageddon,* p. 355)
	The Resurrection of Judgment includes: ". . . those persons whose hearts may have been wanting to do right, but who died without ever having had an opportunity to hear of God's purposes or to learn what He expects of men." *(Paradise Lost,* p. 229) Billions will be brought back for this "resurrection." *(Paradise Lost,* p. 232)	Raised with physical bodies	This resurrection will spread out over a long p riod in the Millennium, that people who have be raised earlier can help to g things ready for those w are yet to return. *(Paradise Lost,* p. 232)

[1]Jehovah's Witnesses teach that there is no soul which survives after death. When a man dies, he totally ceases to exist! *(Paradise Lost,* pp. 293-94) Since these individuals were totally annihilated when they died, the "resurrections" are NEW CREATIONS *(Paradise Lost,* p. 234).

Nathan H. Knorr, Watch Tower President, stops, before leaving a mass ceremony in a Frankfurt, Germany stadium, to give followers a chance to take a picture of him.

CHARLES TAZE RUSSELL
Founder of Jehovah's Witnesses

JOSEPH F. RUTHERFORD-Known as "the Judge," Rutherford was President of The Watch Tower Society from 1917 until his death January 8, 1942.

NATHAN H. KNORR-In 1942, Nathan H. Knorr became the 3rd (and current) President of the Jehovah's Witnesses movement.

new technique that would, by using the patient's blood, reduce the risk of hepatitis. It has been estimated that some 3000 deaths occur every year in the U.S. because of hepatitis contracted from blood transfusions. In fact Dr. Denton Cooley has performed open-heart surgery on Jehovah's Witnesses without transfusion.

THE FLAG SALUTE

Jehovah's Witnesses refuse to salute the flag. In today's world this is not unique. Walk into many school classrooms when the flag salute is in process and you will see many youngsters not saluting the flag...some even showing disrespect by inattention and sitting down.

The Witnesses believe that saluting the flag of any country is an act of idolatry which ascribes salvation to the national emblem and to the nation for which it stands.[23]

A Jehovah's Witness who saluted the flag would, according to their doctrine, be breaking a covenant with God and would be doomed irrevocably. Thus Witness children were forced to choose between persecution and absolute damnation.

MILITARY SERVICE

The Witnesses claim that they are ambassadors of God's kingdom...and, as such, they are neutrals in earthly battles. They also claim exemption from military service because they are ministers.

Joining the military effort of a country in which Witnesses live would result in the Witness "being guilty of desertion and suffering the punishment meted out by Almighty God to deserters."[24]

NO OFFERING PLATES

You will never see an offering plate passed in a Jehovah's Witness meeting. Meetings are held in what they call Kingdom Halls.

In fact, you will never see an elaborate Kingdom Hall. Jehovah's Witness policy is not to waste money on grandiose buildings. Most Kingdom Hall's have a membership of under 200. When they get over this number, another Kingdom Hall is built in a bordering community. The average Kingdom Hall costs about $100 a month to run. An average congregation of 60 people would have to pay about $1.65 per month for the upkeep expenses of their place of worship.

[23]*Let God Be True*, p. 242.
[24]*Let God Be True*, p. 238.

In the August 15, 1971 issue of *The Watchtower* the following note appeared on why they do not believe in passing offering plates:

> The emphasis in all giving among the Witnesses is that it must be voluntary and spontaneous, from the heart. In fact, ever since the earliest days of the modern witnesses of Jehovah it has been their policy that never should there be any passing of collection plates or similar solicitations for money. It was their conviction that this is Jehovah's work and that he would open the hearts of his people to make the necessary contributions so that necessary funds would always be available for the expansion of the preaching of the Gospel.
>
> At all of their meeting places there is a contribution box. Those who want to contribute to the support of the worship by the Witnesses may go to that box and give to the extent that they are able. There are no envelopes, no identification...
>
> Newcomers at the Kingdom Halls of Jehovah's Witnesses are struck with this difference between the way their churches finance their worship and the way Jehovah's Witnesses do. As one woman once put it: "In my church I felt like a dollar sign...But here at Kingdom Hall I was not made to feel that way at all."
>
> Does the place of worship that you attend adhere to these Bible standards regarding religious expenses? If it does not, do you believe that God is pleased with your associating with an organization that disregards the standards of his Word?

Unfortunately, many people, so awed by this "no offering plate" practice join Jehovah's Witnesses at least partially because of this concept. And while the Witnesses say their method of collection is following the "standards of his Word," they incorporate glaring deviations from the Word of God into their doctrine and have become a rapidly growing cult.

It must also be brought to the attention of our readers that those who work at the printing plant in Brooklyn receive only $14 a month as salary. This means the overhead for printing the millions of books and publications each month is at a bare minimum. Their costs are extremely low.

A subscription to *The Watchtower* publication is $1.50 a year. Their books are sold at a low price...the publishing costs are low...and the distribution costs virtually are nothing since the Witnesses sell them as a part of their ministry. With over 7 million copies of *The Watchtower* distributed each week (many at a per copy cost of 5c each), a handsome profit can be realized to carry on the work at Brooklyn headquarters.

Over 81,000 Jehovah's Witnesses are shown in this aerial view of Dodger Stadium in Los Angeles, July, 1969.

Part of record-breaking crown of 194,418 Jehovah's Witnesses who jammed the Polo Grounds and Yankee Stadium, August 1, 1958. At this convention they adopted a resolution condemning "...the religious leaders of Christendom for delinquency, hypocrisy and worldly-wise schemes."

Imagine if you had over 1 MILLION volunteers devoting over 275 MILLION hours in one year (without pay) to sell a publication of yours printed by labor that received only $14 a month...what a tremendous income you could generate!

In one sense of the word, Jehovah's Witnesses are basically a publishing plant. With this in mind, one can see why offering plates need not be passed.

On the other side of the coin, in all fairness, it must be admitted that those who join Jehovah's Witnesses appear to have an untiring zealousness to evangelize the world. And because they believe in what they are doing...they sacrifice personal gain and welcome the opportunity to place their offering in a box at the door.

ORGANIZATION...THAT'S WHAT MAKES THEM TICK

Jehovah's Witnesses are highly organized.

Administration of the over 1,500,000 Jehovah's Witnesses throughout the world radiates from the international headquarters in Brooklyn, New York.

This headquarters operation controls some 100 branches worldwide. Within these branches are over 27,000 congregations and over 91,000 special *full-time* representatives.

In the United States alone there are over 5600 congregations, 340 circuits and 30 total Districts.

There are over 200 congregations in New York City. Every congregation worldwide is assigned specific boundaries of operation.

The branches (over 100) are visited each year by the President of the Watch Tower Bible and Tract Society. When he cannot visit them, he sends one of his "zone servants."

The congregations (over 27,000) are visited about three times a year by a "circuit servant." Most "circuit servants" are responsible for up to 16 congregations. All the congregations in that specific circuit assemble twice a year...at which time they are visited by a "District servant." The "District servant" reaches some 10-12 circuits annually.

This "District servant" reports to the branch office (of which there are about 100)...which in turn reports to the international headquarters at Brooklyn.

This highly organized procedure is the oil that keeps the publishing plant humming and contributes to the growth of this cult.

COMPLEX CORPORATION STRUCTURE

Was it Gertrude Stein who said, "A rose by any other name is still a rose"? The Jehovah's Witnesses organization wears different hats and goes by several names...each created to fill a specific purpose. But regardless of the name changes, it is still a cult...and still propagandizes the "original creations" of its founder, Charles Taze Russell...with additional "revelations" by Joseph Franklin Rutherford.

To carry on their mission they needed a formal organization, one that would be recognized by the governments throughout the world. So, in 1884, the "Watch Tower Bible and Tract Society of Pennsylvania" was chartered. This corporation was created to oversee the work in all the countries and also the printing of *The Watchtower* and other literature.

In addition to the Pennsylvania corporation, there is also the Watchtower Bible and Tract Society of New York, Inc. which was originally chartered in 1909 as the People's Pulpit Association of New York (The name change occurred in 1956). The purpose of this corporation was to purchase and own property.

In addition to these two corporations there are a number of other corporations which include the International Bible Students Association of Canada, the International Bible Students Association of Great Britain and similar societies in different countries.

KINGDOM HALL FUNCTIONS LIKE A COMPUTERIZED PROGRAM

Presiding Ministers

Each congregation of Jehovah's Witnesses has a "presiding minister." He is sometimes referred to as the "congregation servant" or "overseer." His spiritual maturity qualifies him for this position. His duties are to see that all those living in the territory assigned to the congregation receive a regular and thorough witness. His duty also includes seeing that all in the congregation are aided to fulfill their dedication in a "manner acceptable to God." Quota systems for book sales and house to house calls become part of that "fulfillment of dedication."

In 1970 alone, Witnesses devoted some 267,581,120 hours to talking about the Bible and Witness beliefs from house to house. As a result 164,193 persons left their former religious affiliation and joined the Jehovah's Witnesses!

Ministerial Servants
Ministerial Servants are appointed, not merely to assist the Presiding Minister but also to carry out certain duties which can include:

Assistant Congregation Servant
He takes over the service when the Presiding Minister is absent. It is his business to know who is in need of aid because he tabulates the reports turned in by each Witness and keeps accurate records of their ministry. Once a month he sends these reports to the Society's branch office...branch office reports then go to the world headquarters.

Just for a moment, imagine what would happen in your church, if they kept individual reports on your efficiency, how many house calls you made, how many books and pamphlets you sold, how many people you witnessed to each week, how many meetings you attended each week, and how many Bible study groups you attended each week. Most likely, you would soon switch churches, wouldn't you? Not so, however, with the faithful following of Jehovah's Witnesses.

Bible Study Servants
All members of Jehovah's Witness are considered teachers and ministers. After making house to house calls, they take prospective converts who have shown an interest and conduct home Bible studies...and send in their Bible Study Reports at regular intervals. In 1970 1,146,378 *weekly* home Bible studies were conducted throughout the world. The teacher goes directly to the home of the interested individual and they study an assigned Bible subject every week for at least *one hour* for a six-month or 26 week period.

Literature Servants
Jehovah's Witnesses use printed sermons when they teach. The books and booklets used are ordered and cared for by this Literature Servant. Anyone who has entered into a discussion on Bible truths with Jehovah's Witnesses will recognize the fact that they are "programmed" to come up with stock answers following a set pattern. When a Christian asks them questions from Scripture that deviate from their patterned answer, they usually become confused, stop talking or leave. Since the Witnesses have so mangled the precious truths of Scripture with their own contrived creations and the "progressive revelations" of Judge Rutherford, one can see why they must follow a pattern of printed sermons and a canned presentation.

Literature is printed in over 150 languages. Jehovah's Witnesses place over 18 million bound books a year into homes throughout the world...and this rate increases about 10% each year.

This map of the United States in Jehovah's Witnesses headquarters in Brooklyn shows the Districts and their growth. Members of local Kingdom Halls are responsible to cover block by block their territory. As an example, in New York City there are 200 congregations. Each congregation is assigned specific boundaries of operation.

In 1970 the total production of printed material for Bible study amounted to 29,138,291 books and 13,965,784 booklets. This figure does *not* include the *Watchtower* and *Awake* magazines!

Magazine-Territory Servant

The congregation is expected to place numerous copies of each issue of *The Watchtower* and *Awake* in its territory. The Magazine Servant oversees this operation for his local Kingdom Hall. The congregation is assigned a specific territory to cover in its distribution by the international office. The Magazine-Territory Servant assigns portions of that territory to each individual within his congregation.

In 1970 Jehovah's Witnesses obtained 2,464,196 new subscriptions for these magazines. In addition to that, they distributed 204,758,521 individual copies to interested persons who were not subscribers. Besides this, those who purchased individual copies received return visits by the Witnesses. In this activity Jehovah's Witnesses made 121,226,605 return visits on individual homes!

Accounts Servant

Salaries are *not* paid the Presiding Minister nor to his ministerial assistants. There are no collection plates, no tithes, no envelopes, no list of contributors. The Accounts Servant is responsible for paying expenses entailed with maintaining Kingdom Hall and for paying for the literature ordered from Brooklyn headquarters.

Pioneers

Many men and women desire to spend all their time spreading the Jehovah's Witness message. They are called Pioneers and must devote 150 hours or more every month in preaching in the territory they are assigned. There are over 13,500 Pioneers.

Then there is a group who spend 10 to 20 hours a month in this pioneer ministry. There are 1,295,911 such "congregation publishers." There are also 75,455 people who spend about 100 hours a month. This makes a grand total of 1,384,856 on the average engaging in the "pioneer" ministry every month.

SUNDAY is SELLING DAY for KINGDOM HALLS

Jehovah's Witnesses meet either in private homes or in their modest auditorium "Kingdom Halls."

Since congregations are kept small (two congregations being formed from one when it reaches about 200 persons), Kingdom Halls are always moderate in size.

Congregation Book Study

Early in the week Jehovah's Witnesses go to the nearest Kingdom Hall for a one-hour group study using their *New World Translation of the Holy Scriptures* (designed to conform to their theology) and a textbook by the Watch Tower Society.

Theocratic Ministry School

Jehovah's Witnesses are encouraged to "go to school for life." To do this they enroll in the Theocratic Ministry School that is held at their Kingdom Hall one evening each week. This is a *perpetual* training school for men, women and children. This trains them primarily for their house to house visitation.

Service Meeting

Usually on the same evening as the Theocratic Ministry School the congregation holds their weekly Service Meeting. A monthly pamphlet issued from Brooklyn headquarters guides their thinking for the week and could be compared to a "sales tip sheet" to help the Witnesses up their quota of book sales. A variety of speakers discuss and demonstrate new door-to-door sermons, how to increase and follow up placements of Bible literature and how to improve their presentation ability.

Public Meeting

Most congregations use Sunday morning for house-to-house preaching. It is not until afternoon or evening that the entire congregation assembles at the Kingdom Hall for the weekly public meeting and *Watchtower study.*

Watchtower Study

The Sunday Public Meeting is generally followed by what Jehovah's Witnesses call their most important congregation meeting...the WATCHTOWER STUDY. This is a question and answer discussion on subjects found in the current issue of *The Watchtower.*

PUBLISHING...THE HEART AND SUCCESS OF THE JEHOVAH'S WITNESS MOVEMENT

Jehovah's Witnesses have learned a secret that most Christian groups have yet to learn...PUBLISH...PUBLISH...PUBLISH.

There is no doubt that the pen is MIGHTIER...and the printed word is so much more effective and more lasting than the spoken word. And while this should be public knowledge it seems that the cults are just about the only ones who have taken advantage of this fact. (Herbert W. Armstrong's Church of God publishes over 3 million magazines and booklets a month. One is THE PLAIN TRUTH.)

By 1919 Jehovah's Witnesses began their own printing in Brooklyn. It all started with a little job press in a room under the kitchen. Since then it has grown into 4 large buildings where printing presses gobble up 8 freight carloads of paper per week...over 10,000 tons per year!

The first printing factory of the Society consisted of 3 floors. Later on, in 1927, an 8 story factory was built at 117 Adams Street in Brooklyn. Within 10 years space was so cramped that a 4-story addition was built. This only lasted 9 years. Then a 9-story addition was made that would double its floor space! Within 4 more years, because of the phenomenal growth of the Witnesses, another additional 13-story building was erected.

Let's take a brief walk through these factories:

No. 1 Factory Building

Here are folders and stitchers that can stitch 100,000 32-page booklets per day! About 20 rotary and two flatbed presses are on the 6th floor. The large presses each print 25,000 magazines an hour, and they weigh over 50 tons. Each rotary press cost more than $400,000! They use a 5-mile-long, 1600 pound roll of paper. Literature is printed in over 150 languages. Twenty-five other languages are printed in foreign lands. In Japan, in 1970, they printed 7,400,000 magazines alone!

In this building the Witnesses manufacture their own paint, build their own furniture for the Headquarters building and produce their own electricity to run their machinery and presses. They also manufacture their own paste and glue.

No. 2 Factory Building

Here address plates are maintained—with over 1½ million stencils. Magazines are wrapped and mailed from here. Some rotary presses are also located here...as well as a well-equipped machine shop.

No. 3 Factory Building

Two floors in this building are designed to hold 23 rotary presses. The bindery in this building has the capacity to bind 50,000 books a day.

All shipping is done from this building. Over 50% of all of the literature produced is exported to foreign parts of the world.

If all of the over 10 million bound books and Bibles produced in one year at the Watchtower printing plant were stacked one on top of the other...they would make a stack over 450 times the height of the Empire State Building.

They are diligent planners. They keep a two-year *advance* supply of literature stored up in branch locations throughout the world in case of a strike or conflict.

Each Jehovah's Witness works 5½ days per week, 8 hours and 40 minutes per weekday, at these plants. All those who live at "Bethel," the headquarters hotel in Brooklyn, receive food and shelter and an allowance of $14 a month for personal necessities. When they travel to other parts of New York to do their "witnessing," their carfare money comes out of the $14 a month. Even Nathan Homer Knorr, President of the Watch Tower Society receives under $20 per month!

DETERMINED DEDICATION

The heart of the Witness movement is at Bethel, the Watch Tower Society headquarters. Here are not only the Administration offices, but the training school for selected "ministers" is also on this site.

The brothers and sisters willingly do menial work to keep the operation humming. Some press 150 shirts an hour, 6000 a week. Some help serve the over 150 gallons of coffee consumed each week....all for $14 a month!

To spur them on there are signs on the factory floor above the exit doors which advise them whether they are

1 DAY BEHIND SCHEDULE
or
1 DAY AHEAD OF SCHEDULE

and to maintain their rigid schedule of determined dedication and unswerving devotion they still follow Charles Taze Russell's advice to

Eat breakfast like a king
Eat lunch like a prince
but
Eat dinner like a pauper

And just in the time it took you to read this book, faithful Jehovah's Witnesses were

(1) Distributing 56,250 magazines
(2) Making 30,306 return calls to interested prospects
(3) Converting 41 more people to their cult

Perhaps it might be instructive for us here to read pages 33 and 34 of the 1971 *Yearbook of Jehovah's Witnesses:*

> There is a great difference between those persons who belong to Christendom's religions and Jehovah's witnesses. Christendom requires little or nothing of their members except to make contributions to the church. At Christmas and Easter time much larger numbers than usual attend the church services...
>
> There is no dedication of people's lives to the doing of God's will, or walking in the footsteps of Jesus Christ. The church members of both Catholic and Protestant denominations, as well as their clergy, do not know anymore what Jesus meant when he said: "Go therefore and make disciples of people of all nations, baptizing them...teaching them to observe all the things I have commanded you" (Matthew 28:19,20).
>
> This was no meaningless statement on the part of Christ Jesus. He meant that every follower of his should be a witness of him wherever he lives...That is how Jehovah's witnesses feel about it. They take their commission seriously...

Quite challenging words aren't they? How much more should we who are Christians and know God's Word...who know truth from error...and who know the error of Jehovah's Witness theology...be dedicated to our King and soon coming Lord.

How can I do less, than give Him my best...
And live for Him completely,
After all He's done for me!

REMEMBER...

As Edmond Charles Gruss has so aptly put it, Jehovah's Witnesses are Apostles of Denial. They DENY:

1. The Trinity
2. The Deity of Christ
3. The personality of the Holy Spirit
4. The inherent immortality of the soul
5. The total depravity of man
6. The bodily resurrection of Christ
7. The atonement
8. The finished work of Christ and the need of the new birth
9. The Second Coming of Christ
10. Eternal punishment

... plus a host of other denials of Bible truth.

How important it is for us as Christians to recognize the Jehovah's Witnesses as another false cult. And God's Word, the Bible, tells us, "...from such turn away." (2 Timothy 3:5,7)

JEHOVAH'S WITNESSES on the DEITY OF CHRIST

(Jehovah's Witnesses classify Christ into 3 different states: Prehuman, Human and Posthuman.)

PREHUMAN STATE

Prior to coming to earth, this only-begotten Son of God did not think himself to be co-equal with Jehovah God; he did not view himself as "equal in power and glory" with Almighty God... (*Let God Be True*, p. 34).

Did this firstborn Son possess immortality, that is, deathlessness? That he did not have this quality and was not immortal at that time is proved by later facts as well as plainly stated in the Bible.... The time came, however that Jehovah God opened up to his Son the opportunity to gain immortality. (*The Truth Shall Make You Free*, p. 44)

(This prehuman state, according to Jehovah's Witnesses, lasted from the time of the Son's creation to the time when he was born of Mary. Jehovah's Witnesses insist that at no time was the Son equal to Jehovah. They say that prior to the Son's coming to earth as a man, he was not known in heaven as Jesus Christ, but as Michael, the archangel.)

THE BIBLE on the DEITY OF CHRIST

PREHUMAN STATE

And now, O Father, glorify thou Me with thine own self with the glory which I had with thee before the world was.(John17:5)

Christ existed before His incarnation in a state of glory shared with the Father.

"Incarnation" is from the Latin, meaning "becoming flesh," that is, "becoming human." The doctrine of the incarnation teaches that the eternal Son of God became human, and that He did so without in any manner or degree diminishing His divine nature.

But thou, Bethlehem Ephrathah, though thou be little among the thousands of Judah, yet out of thee shall He come forth unto me that is to be ruler in Israel, whose goings forth have been from of old, from everlasting. (Micah 5:2)

Micah, 700 years before Christ came, predicted that the Messiah would be born in Bethlehem. Note that the words, "whose goings have been from of old, from everlasting," prove that the Messiah, Christ, existed from eternity past—"from everlasting."

...I am the first and the last.

(Revelation 1:17)

I am Alpha and Omega, the beginning and the end, the first and the last.

(Revelation 22:13)

Christ's claims to be the Alpha and Omega, the first and the last, in time and in every matter, can only be construed as a claim of deity and of His eternal past and future existence. The "first" does not mean the "second"—which would be the case if He were created as an angelic creature when the Father already existed as the "first." In acknowledging Christ's deity we only affirm of Him what He here claims.

JEHOVAH'S WITNESSES on the DEITY OF CHRIST

HUMAN STATE

(Christ was not God in the flesh, say Jehovah's Witnesses)

If a mere incarnation of the Son of God had been intended, then it would not have been necessary for him to have his life transferred to an embryo in the virgin's womb and to be developed there and finally born as a helpless infant. He could still have remained a spirit person and materialized a fully developed fleshly body and clothed himself with it...
(*Religion for Mankind*, p. 231)

Actually, however, what is here described is not an incarnation but a temporary assumption of a body for the purpose of bringing a message.
(*The Truth Shall Make You Free*, p. 245)

By pouring out his holy spirit upon the baptized Jesus, God anointed him with the spirit to be the long-promised King...Jesus became the Messiah...
(*Let God Be True*, p. 38)

It was at his baptism that Jesus was "born again."
(*The Watchtower*, 75-681, November 15, 1954)

The very fact that he was sent proves he was not equal with God but less than God the Father.
(*"The Word" Who Is He?*, p. 41)

The BIBLE on the DEITY OF CHRIST

HUMAN STATE

Therefore the Lord Himself shall give you a sign; Behold the virgin shall conceive, and bear a son, and shall call His name Immanuel. *(Isaiah 7:14)*

Christ's symbolic name, *Immanuel*, in the Hebrew literally means, "God with us." Truly it is the Bible, not men, that has brought to us the doctrine of the deity of Christ.

The first man is of the earth, earthy; the second man is the Lord from heaven.
(I Corinthians 15:47)

Paul here compares Adam with Christ. In doing so he asserts Christ's deity.

For unto us a child is born, unto us a son is given: and the government shall be upon His shoulder: and His name shall be called Wonderful, Counselor, The Mighty God, The everlasting Father, The Prince of Peace. *(Isaiah 9:6)*

Isaiah saw that the Messiah was to be both human and divine—so that He could: (1) as one of our own Adamic human race suffer for our sins, and (2) as deity His death could provide the infinite sinless sacrifice necessary to pay for the sin committed by the sinners for whom His death would atone. Thus Isaiah sees Him both as "a child" and as "The mighty God, The Everlasting Father."

But Jesus answered them, My Father worketh hitherto, and I work.

Therefore, the Jews sought the more to kill Him, because He not only had broken the sabbath, but said also that God was His Father, making Himself equal with God. *(John 5:17-18)*

John here gives us the truth of the matter—the Pharisees perceived in Christ's words a claim to equality with God. If Jesus were not equal with God right here He could have cleared this matter up. Not only could He have

The BIBLE on the DEITY OF CHRIST

HUMAN STATE (continued)

cleared it up, but it would have been sin on His part not to have denied at once that He was claiming equality with God—unless He actually did claim it. He did claim it and we believe it, although the Pharisees then and the Jehovah's Witnesses today are offended by this claim.

We reject the Jehovah's Witness claim that Jesus' having been "sent" by the Father proves His inequality with God. If in a spirit of perfect agreement and love the wife of the President of the United States sends the President to perform a mutually desired chore—such as to help their daughter—this in no way proves the President's essential inferiority to the First Lady. So here too, Christ's deity is in no way lessened by His being sent by the Father.

At least 8 freight carloads of paper are used per week in this printing plant. Each roll is 1600 pounds and is 5 miles long.

JEHOVAH'S WITNESSES on the DEITY OF CHRIST

POSTHUMAN STATE

(Jehovah's Witnesses reject the bodily resurrection of Christ)

Jehovah God raised Christ from the dead not as a human Son, but as a mighty immortal spirit Son.
(*Let God Be True*, p. 40)

Whether it (his body) was dissolved into gases or whether it is still preserved somewhere as the grand memorial of God's love, of Christ's obedience, and of our redemption, no one knows...
(*Studies in the Scriptures*, II, p. 129)

Usually they could not at first tell it was Jesus, for he appeared in different bodies. He appeared and disappeared just as angels had done, because he was resurrected as a spirit creature. Only because Thomas would not believe did Jesus appear in a body like that in which he died.
(*From Paradise Lost to Paradise Regained*, p. 144)

(Since Jehovah's Witnesses believe that Christ's resurrection was a spiritual one...they explain away his bodily post-resurrection appearances.)

The BIBLE on the DEITY OF CHRIST

POSTHUMAN STATE

And, after eight days, again His disciples were inside, and Thomas with them; then came Jesus, the doors being shut, and stood in the midst, and said, Peace be unto you.

Then saith He to Thomas, Reach here thy finger, and behold My hands; and reach here thy hand, and thrust it into My side and be not faithless, but believing.

(John 20:26-27)

But they were terrified and frightened, and supposed that they had seen a spirit.

And He said unto them, Why are ye troubled? And why do thoughts arise in your hearts?

Behold My hands and My feet, that it is I myself; handle Me, and see; for a spirit hath not flesh and bones, as ye see Me have.

And when He had thus spoken, He showed them His hands and His feet.

And while they yet believed not for joy, and wondered, He said unto them, Have ye here anything to eat?

And they gave Him a piece of a broiled fish, and a honeycomb.

And He took it, and did eat before them.

(Luke24:37-43)

Jesus declared, "*...a spirit hath not flesh and bones, as ye see Me have.*"These words render futile all Jehovah's Witness claims and long explanations denying that Christ rose in a literal body, and in the same body in which He was crucified.

Jesus' eating before them can only be construed as His clear-cut attempt to convince them thoroughly that He had arisen in a body and not as a mere spirit. The Jehovah's Witness suggestion that He arose merely as a spirit, but only temporarily took on a body only to convince Thomas, must be rejected. The whole tenor of Jesus' words constitutes His appeal to us to believe that He was not raised as a spirit, but rather in His

JEHOVAH'S WITNESSES on the DEITY OF CHRIST

POSTHUMAN STATE (continued)

(Jehovah's Witnesses believe that none but God had immortality. Christ was given immortality at his resurrection...)

Christ Jesus was first to receive immortality as a reward for his faithful course on earth....
(*Let God Be True*, p. 74)

The Son now resumed the name Michael to tie him with his prehuman existence.
(*Your Will Be Done*, p. 316)

God exalted his son Jesus to be higher than he was before he lived and died as a man...Jesus is made the Head under Jehovah of God's capital organization over the entire Universe.
(*Let God Be True*, p. 40)

The BIBLE on the DEITY OF CHRIST

POSTHUMAN STATE (continued)

crucified physical human body.

Shall we believe Christ or Russell and Rutherford?

But thou, Bethlehem Ephrathah, though thou be little among the thousands of Judah, yet out of thee shall He come forth unto Me that is to be ruler in Israel, whose goings forth have been from of old, from everlasting. *(Micah 5:2)*

The Prophet saw that the Christ was to be born a human—coming from Bethlehem—but yet He was eternal—"...whose goings forth have been from of old, everlasting." One who is "from everlasting" does not "receive immortality"—as claimed by the Jehovah's Witnesses. He is immortal!

Yet Michael the archangel, when contending with the devil he disputed about the body of Moses, durst not bring against him a railing accusation, but said, The Lord rebuke thee. *(Jude 9)*

Michael is here declared to be an archangel. The identification of Michael, an angelic being, hence a *created* being, with Jesus, the creator of all (John 1:1-3) is totally without Biblical support or evidence.

God, who at sundry times and in divers manners spake in time past unto the fathers by the prophets,

Hath in these last days spoken unto us by His Son, whom He hath appointed heir of all things, by whom also He made the worlds.

Who being the brightness of His glory, and the express image of His person, and upholding all things by the word of His power, when He had by Himself purged our sins, sat down on the right hand of the Majesty on high.

Being made so much better than the angels, as He hath by inheritance obtained a more excellent name than they.
(Hebrews1:1-4)

The BIBLE on the
DEITY OF CHRIST

POSTHUMAN STATE
(continued)

Here we have the express declaration that Christ is superior to *all* angelic creatures, which includes archangels—for "head-angels" are still angels. Christ being "*...so much better than the angels...*" cannot then be Michael who is after all, according to Jude 9, an angel.

In fact, the whole argument of Hebrews, chapter 1 is meant to prove Christ to be above all angels, and hence not Himself an angelic creature.

Thus the Jehovah's Witness assertion that Christ is the angel Michael must be seen to be another man-made imagination which runs counter to the evidence of the Scriptures.

See Philippians 2:5-7; Revelation 22:8-9 compared to Philippians 2:10; and Psalm 110:1 for further evidence on the deity of Christ.

In his excellent book, *The Four Major Cults* (William B. Eerdmans Publishing Company, 1963), Anthony A. Hoekama provides a penetrating conclusion to the study of the Deity of Christ as viewed by the Jehovah's Witnesses. He says, ...what the three states of Christ's existence in Watchtower theology really amount to is this:

angel — man — angel

with no real continuity between the three. A little reflection will reveal how devastating this view is to the Christology of the Scriptures. The individual who laid down his life at Calvary was not the individual who existed previously in heaven and was God's agent in creation: the individual who is now ruling over his heavenly Kingdom is not the individual who died on the cross for us.

Really, Jehovah's Witnesses have three Christs, none whom is equal to Jehovah, and none of whom is the Christ of the Scriptures.

JEHOVAH'S WITNESSES on the TRINITY

The doctrine of the trinity had its origin in the demon-religions of ancient Babylon, India, and Egypt. The obvious conclusion is, therefore, that Satan is the originator of the Trinity doctrine.
(*Let God Be True*, p. 101)

...Sincere persons who want to know the true God and serve Him find it a bit difficult to love and worship a complicated...freakish-looking, three-headed God.
(*Let God Be True*, p. 102)

The trinity doctrine was not conceived by Jesus or the early Christians. The plain truth is that this is another of Satan's attempts to keep God-fearing persons from learning the truth of Jehovah and His Son, Christ Jesus. No, there is no trinity!
(*Let God Be True*, p. 111)

The Holy Spirit is therefore neither God nor a person; he is merely an impersonal force.
(*Let Your Name Be Sanctified*, p. 269)

The BIBLE on the TRINITY

The word *Trinity* is a short form for *Tri-unity*.

This is the Biblically based doctrine that the true God is One God (Deuteronomy 6:4), a *Unity*, and yet at the same time this One God is manifest in three, *Tri-*, divine persons.

Thus there is only One God, not 3 gods, but the One Godhead consists of the Father, the Son, and the Holy Spirit, three co-divine, co-eternal persons.

That this is a complex mystery should surprise no one—for God is unfathomable.

The standard proof of the trinity runs as follows:

1. The Godhead is One. (Deuteronomy 6:4)

2a. The Father is a Person; (John17:3)

2b. The Father is Divine; (John 17:3)

2c. Hence, the Father is a Divine Person.

3a. The Son is a Person; (Matthew 17:5)

3b. The Son is Divine (as well as human); (John 5:17-18; 17:5; Philippians 2:5-6)

3c. Hence, the Son is a Divine Person.

4a. The Holy Spirit is a Person; (John 14:16, 17, 26; 15:26; Ephesians 4:30) (He, as a person, can be "grieved")

4b. The Holy Spirit is Divine; (Matthew 12:31-32) (He, as God, can be blasphemed against)

4c. Hence, the Holy Spirit is a Divine Person.

5. Hence, the Godhead is a Tri-unity, one Godhead composed of three Divine Persons.

That this is the teaching of the Bible has been affirmed by the Church universal from the first ecumenical councils onward (The Council of Nicea, 325 A.D.; the First Council of Constantinople, 381 A.D.).

The trinity is further affirmed by the Scripture's mentioning and elevating all Three of the Persons together within the

JEHOVAH'S WITNESSES on SALVATION

(Jehovah's Witnesses break up their Society into two classes: (1) *The Congregation of God*...sometimes referred to as "the Annointed class," "the Elect," "the Kingdom Class," "the Little Flock," "the Chosen Ones," and "Spiritual Israel"....and "the 144,000." (2) *The Other Sheep*...sometimes referred to as "Great Company," "Great Multitude," "Great Crowd," and "Jonadabs").

THE ANOINTED CLASS

(The Witnesses believe in the New Birth but it is an exclusive privilege made available only to Christ and the select 144,000, the Anointed Class).

Long ago Jehovah determined that the Christians who will make up this spiritual nation would be very few in number. Of those who make up God's spiritual nation (spiritual Israel), the Bible says that they are "the 144,000, who have been purchased from the earth" (Revelation 14:3). So from among mankind only 144,000 persons will ever go to heaven.

When the "time of the end" began in 1914 the full number that was needed to make up God's spiritual nation (144,000) was not yet complete. More had to be gathered. This meant preaching. Rightly, the ones to do this preaching must be Jehovah's witnesses...By means of this preaching the last ones that were needed to fill the number of God's spiritual nation would be gathered from the nations.

(*From Paradise Lost to Paradise Regained*, p. 186)

The BIBLE on SALVATION

But as many as received Him, to them gave He power to become the sons of God, even to them that believe on His name:

Which were born, not of blood, nor of the will of the flesh, nor of the will of man, but of God. *(John 1:12-13)*

Verily, verily, I say unto you, He that heareth My word, and believeth on Him that sent Me, hath everlasting life, and shall not come into judgment but is passed from death unto life. *(John 5:24)*

Jesus said unto her, I am the resurrection, and the life; He that believeth in Me, though he were dead, yet shall he live.

And whosoever liveth and believeth in Me shall never die. Believest thou this? *(John 11:25-26)*

Repent, therefore, and be converted, that your sins may be blotted out... *(Acts 3:19)*

And they said, Believe on the Lord Jesus Christ, and thou shalt be saved, and thy house. *(Acts 16:31)*

For I am not ashamed of the gospel of Christ; for it is the power of God unto salvation to everyone that believeth; to the Jew first, and also to the Greek. *(Romans 1:16)*

That if thou shalt confess with thy mouth the Lord Jesus, and shalt believe in thine heart that God hath raised Him from the dead, thou shalt be saved.

For with the heart man believeth unto righteousness; and with the mouth confession is made unto salvation. *(Romans 10:9-10)*

For by grace are ye saved through faith; and that not of yourselves, it is the gift of God—Not of works, lest any man should boast. *(Ephesians 2:8-9)*

The reader should carefully compare the above quoted sample Scriptures with the complex jargon of the Jehovah's Witnesses. Repent and believe (trust Jesus as the one who died for your sins) is the universal Biblical appeal to all sinners in all ages.

JEHOVAH'S WITNESSES on SALVATION

THE ANOINTED CLASS (continued)

(The Anointed Ones must preach the good news of Christ's Kingdom. If they maintain their integrity until death they will receive immortality. If they turn back from this dedication, such turning back "would mark them as agreement-breakers, worthy of death, annihilation.")
(*Let God Be True*, p. 301)

(Thus, while Jehovah's Witnesses claim that salvation is of grace...it is not really God's sovereign grace that saves even the 144,000, but rather man who saves himself by grasping the ransom by dedicated works.)

The BIBLE on SALVATION

(continued)

Man-invented Jehovah Witness requirements and class divisions among the saved (Jonadabs; Anointed Class, etc.) are alike foreign to the simple straightforward Bible appeal for all sinners to come to Jesus by faith alone for forgiveness.

If the Jehovah's Witness doctrine of "maintaining their integrity" by works is the standard, John 18 and Galatians 2, quoted below, show that not even Peter nor Barnabas could remain saved—which is an unfathomable absurdity.

Then saith the maid that kept the door unto Peter, Art not thou also one of this man's disciples? He saith, I am not.

And Simon Peter stood and warmed himself. They said, therefore unto him, Art not thou also one of His disciples? He denied it, and said, I am not.

One of the servants of the high priest, being his kinsman whose ear Peter cut off, saith, Did not I see thee in the garden with Him?

Peter then denied again; and immediately the cock crowed. (John 18:17, 25-27)

But when Peter was come to Antioch, I withstood him to the face, because he was to be blamed.

For before certain men came from James, he did eat with the Gentiles; but when they were come, he withdrew and separated himself, fearing them who were of the circumcision.

And the other Jews dissembled in like manner with him, insomuch that Barnabas also was carried away with their false pretense.

But when I saw that they walked not uprightly according to the truth of the gospel, I said unto Peter before them all, If thou, being a Jew, livest after the manner of Gentiles, and not as do the Jews, why compellest thou the Gentiles to

JEHOVAH'S WITNESSES on SALVATION
THE ANOINTED CLASS
(continued)

The BIBLE on SALVATION
(continued)

live as do the Jews?

We who are Jews by nature and not sinners of the Gentiles,

Knowing that a man is not justified by the works of the law, but by the faith of Jesus Christ, even we have believed in Jesus Christ, that we might be justified by the faith of Christ, and not by the works of the law; for by the works of the law shall no flesh be justified. (Galatians 2:11-16)

Faith in Christ saves. Good works neither get anyone saved nor do they keep anyone saved. They, good works, are rather the product of salvation—not its cause nor condition.

One of the many enlightening truths that God now gave his witnesses was about the members of God's spiritual nation who had died physically. This was in 1927. In that year the witnesses understood that the dead spiritual Israelites had been raised in 1918 to live in heaven with Christ Jesus. It was an invisible resurrection, of course.

From 1918 on, when one of the last ones of God's spiritual nation dies, he does not have to sleep in death. At death God raises him to life in heaven...Less than 20,000 of the last ones of God's spiritual nation are now left on earth.
(*From Paradise Lost to Paradise Regained*, p. 192)

Once a person decides that the Bible is his or her only inspired fountain of truth from God, that person sees all of the Jehovah's Witness divisions pivoting on such dates as 1914, 1918, and 1927 as so much man-made mumbo-jumbo. It is completely and totally unbiblical.

And I heard the number of them which were sealed; and there were sealed an hundred and forty and four thousand of all the tribes of the children of Israel.

Of the tribe of Judah were sealed twelve thousand. Of the tribe of Reuben were sealed twelve thousand. Of the tribe of Gad were sealed twelve thousand.

Of the tribe of Asher were sealed twelve

JEHOVAH'S WITNESSES on SALVATION

(continued)

THE OTHER SHEEP
(The Great Crowd)

(According to Jehovah Witness doctrine, only the select 144,000 need to be born again..since they and they only will go to Heaven. The other Witnesses do not need this new birth.)

The "Great Crowd" are not "born again," nor do they need to be "born again," because they gain everlasting life on the earth.
(*The Watchtower*, 75:682, November 15, 1954)

To gain paradise and life Jehovah's Witnesses list 4 steps:

1. Study the Bible
2. Association with the Witnesses is essential to salvation
3. Change your living from the former way to God's way
4. You must also be a preacher and a witness. "Only the preachers of God's kingdom can expect to be protected during the end of this world and to live through Armageddon into the new world."

(*Paradise Lost to Paradise Regained*, p. 242, 244, 246, 249)

Justification comes to THE OTHER SHEEP by their "unbreakable steadfastness" during the Millennium.

The BIBLE ON SALVATION

(continued)

thousand. Of the tribe of Naphtali were sealed twelve thousand. Of the tribe of Manasseh were sealed twelve thousand.

Of the tribe of Simeon were sealed twelve thousand. Of the tribe of Levi were sealed twelve thousand. Of the tribe of Issachar were sealed twelve thousand.

Of the tribe of Zebulun were sealed twelve thousand. Of the tribe of Joseph were sealed twelve thousand. Of the tribe of Benjamin were sealed twelve thousand.
(Revelation7:4-8)

The Mormons claim that the American Indians of the southwest are of Israelite lineage. Herbert W. and Garner Ted Armstrong, British-Israelites, see England, the United States, and northwestern Europe as the nations of these tribes.

Now, the Jehovah's Witnesses claim them to be the converts to Jehovah's Witnesses in their early 1914 on to the 1920's era. Who next will claim the 144,000?

The Bible calls them Israelites and names their tribes. Thus these are exactly what the Bible says—Israelites, Jews, Hebrews from the tribes—in the end-time when God again calls Israel to Himself in conversion to Christ.

That if thou shalt confess with thy mouth the Lord Jesus, and shalt believe in thine heart that God hath raised Him from the dead, thou shalt be saved.

For with the heart man believeth unto righteousness; and with the mouth confession is made unto salvation.
(Romans 10:9-10)

For by grace are ye saved through faith; and that not of yourselves, it is the gift of God—Not of works, lest any man should boast. *(Ephesians 2:8-9)*

The man-made Jehovah's Witness formulas for finding salvation are foreign to the Bible's appeal to the sinner to come to Christ for forgiveness by faith alone.

JEHOVAH'S WITNESSES on THE LAST THINGS

ON 1914 AND 1918

(Jehovah's Witnesses believe the first official presence of Christ began with his baptism in Jordan and continued until his death 3½ years later.)

This second presence of Christ the Messiah was to be invisible and the unmistakable sign he gave shows conclusively that this return of Christ began in the year 1914. Since that time Christ has turned his attention toward earth's affairs and is dividing the people and educating the true Christians in preparation for their survival during the great storm of Armageddon....
(*Make Sure of All Things*, p. 319)

The year 1914 also marked that time when Satan was cast out of heaven to the earth, and the end of the Gentile times.
(*Let God Be True*, p. 201, 202)

The Bible term "end of the world" means, here, a new time period, the "time of the end" of this old world. This time period had its beginning in 1914; it will close when this world ends in destruction. So 1914 marked the beginning of the "time of the end" for this world.
(*From Paradise Lost to Paradise Regained*, p. 174)

The BIBLE on THE LAST THINGS

ON 1914 AND 1918

But of that day and hour knoweth no man, no, not the angels of heaven, but My Father only.

Watch, therefore; for ye know not what hour your Lord doth come.

But know this, that if the householder had known in what watch the thief would come, he would have watched, and would not have allowed his house to be broken into.

Therefore be ye also ready; for in such an hour as ye think not the Son of man cometh. *(Matthew 24:36, 42-44)*

But of that day and that hour knoweth no man, no, not the angels who are in heaven, neither the Son, but the Father.

Take heed, watch and pray; for ye know not when the time is.

For the Son of man is like a man taking a far journey, who left his house, and gave authority to his servants, and to every man his work, and commanded the porter to watch.

Watch ye, therefore; for ye know not when the master of the house cometh, at evening, or at midnight, or at cockcrow, or in the morning;

Lest, coming suddenly, he find you sleeping.

And what I say unto you I say unto all, Watch. *(Mark 13:32-37)*

The above Scriptures make it abundantly clear that no one living—Charles Taze Russell or anyone else—knows the time of Christ's Second Coming.

For the Lord Himself shall descend from heaven with a shout, with the voice of the archangel, and with the trump of God: and the dead in Christ shall rise first:

Then we which are alive and remain shall be caught up together with them in the clouds to meet the Lord in the air: and so shall we ever be with the Lord.

(I Thessalonians 4:16-17)

JEHOVAH'S WITNESSES on THE LAST THINGS

ON 1914 AND 1918 (continued)

(In 1914, according to Jehovah's Witnesses, Christ was crowned as king...and in 1918 he cleansed Jehovah's spiritual temple. The "spiritual temple" was the Jehovah's Witness earthly organization.)

He came to the spiritual temple as Jehovah's Messenger and began to cleanse it...That marked the beginning of the period of judgment and inspection of his spirit-begotten followers.
(*Let God Be True*, p. 202)

The BIBLE on THE LAST THINGS

ON 1914 AND 1918 (continued)

Did anything like the coming of Christ in the Scriptures quoted on the previous page occur in 1914? Of course not! Christ simply did not come in 1914 despite all the long explanations by the Jehovah's Witnesses. Christ's Second Coming is yet future.

And the Jews' passover was at hand, and Jesus went up to Jerusalem,

And found in the temple those that sold oxen and sheep and doves, and the changers of money, sitting.

And when He had made a scourge of small cords, He drove them all out of the temple, and the sheep, and the oxen; and poured out the changers' money, and overthrew the tables;

And said unto them that sold doves, Take these things from here; make not My Father's house an house of merchandise.

And His disciples remembered that it was written, The zeal of thine house hath eaten Me up. *(John 2:13-17)*

Jesus cleansed the earthly Temple as described in John 2. There is neither Biblical prophecy nor hint alluding to His cleansing any Jehovah's Witness Spiritual Temple in 1918.

It is entirely a man-made claim.

JEHOVAH'S WITNESSES on THE LAST THINGS

THE BATTLE OF ARMAGEDDON

Many people alive since 1914 will still be living when Armageddon begins.
(*Paradise Lost*, p. 205)

Actual combat against Satan and his demon horde began with Christ's enthronement in A.D. 1914. This combat was cut short in A.D. 1918, to be resumed at Armageddon.
(*Make Sure of All Things*, p. 390)

Just before Armageddon begins, the devil will attack the New World Society.
(*Paradise Lost*, p. 205)

The BIBLE on THE LAST THINGS

THE BATTLE OF ARMAGEDDON

The Witnesses claim that "many" people alive in 1914 will live to see Armageddon. This foolish unbiblical time-setting is again running out on them.

Unless Armageddon occurs soon this Jehovah's Witnesses prophecy, of "many" alive in 1914 yet alive to see it, will be proven to be utterly false.

And there was war in heaven; Michael and his angels fought against the dragon, and the dragon fought and his angels,

And prevailed not, neither was their place found any more in heaven.

Therefore rejoice, ye heavens, and ye that dwell in them. Woe to the inhabiters of the earth and of the sea! For the devil is come down unto you, having great wrath, because he knowest that he hath but a short time.

And when the dragon saw that he was cast unto the earth, he persecuted the woman who brought forth the male child.

(Revelation 12:7-8, 12-13)

The Bible (quoted above) nowhere tells exactly when the final battle between Satan and the forces of God begins.

The Jehovah's Witness dates of 1914 and 1918 are pure unsupported imagination.

And He said unto them, It is not for you to know the times or the seasons, which the Father hath put in His own power.

(Acts 1:7)

JEHOVAH'S WITNESSES on THE LAST THINGS

THE BATTLE OF ARMAGEDDON (continued)

(Because it is believed that only those who are members of the Watchtower organization, whether as annointed ones or other sheep, will survive Armageddon, Jehovah's Witnesses preach with great urgency: Come into Jehovah's theocratic organization now, or be forever annihilated in the Battle of Armageddon!)
(*Paradise Lost*, p. 210; *You May Survive Armageddon*, pages 217, 347; *Paradise Lost*, p. 202; *Let God Be True*, pages 260, 261.)

Not a single human being who was against Jehovah's organization will survive.
(*You May Survive Armageddon*, p. 342)

This battle is the most terrific war of all time, in which Jehovah will remove all wickedness from the universe.
(*You May Survive Armageddon into God's New World*, p. 30)

The BIBLE on THE LAST THINGS

THE BATTLE OF ARMAGEDDON (continued)

And it shall come to pass, in that day, that I will seek to destroy all the nations that come against Jerusalem.

And I will pour upon the house of David, and upon the inhabitants of Jerusalem, the Spirit of grace and of supplications; and they shall look upon Me whom they have pierced, and they shall mourn for Him, as one mourneth for his only son, and shall be in bitterness for Him, as one that is in bitterness for his firstborn.

In that day there shall be a fountain opened to the house of David and to the inhabitants of Jerusalem for sin and for uncleanness. (Zechariah 12:9-10; 13:1)

The above passage shows the final conversion of the nation of Israel at Christ's coming at Armageddon.

These Jews survive Armageddon—and there is no hint in the whole Bible that even one of them is a Jehovah's Witness!

And I saw the beast, and the kings of the earth, and their armies, gathered together to make war against Him that sat on the horse, and against His army.

And the beast [Antichrist] was taken, and with him the false prophet that wrought

JEHOVAH'S WITNESSES on THE LAST THINGS
THE BATTLE OF ARMAGEDDON (continued)

It will completely destroy the invisible and visible parts of Satan's world and thus it will spell the accomplished end of this wicked old world. It will be the climax of the tribulation which Jesus predicted.
(*Let God Be True*, p. 259)

Christ will lead heavenly armies of powerful angels. The Jehovah's Witnesses will have no part in fighting the battle.
(*From Paradise Lost to Paradise Regained*, pages 204, 205)

The BIBLE on THE LAST THINGS
THE BATTLE OF ARMAGEDDON (continued)

miracles before him, with which he deceived them that had received the mark of the beast, and them that worshiped his image. These both were cast alive into a lake of fire burning with brimstone.

And the remnant were slain with the sword of Him that sat upon the horse, which sword proceeded out of His mouth; and all the fowls were filled with their flesh. *(Revelation 19:19-21)*

The above Revelation 19 passage shows that *the armies* gathered to Armageddon in *Palestine* will be slain at Christ's coming at the end of the Tribulation Period.

The mass of humanity still alive around the world will then stand in judgement before the now returned Christ (Matthew 25).

When the Son of man shall come in His glory, and all the holy angels with Him, then shall He sit upon the throne of His glory.

And before Him shall be gathered all the nations; and He shall separate them one from another, as a shepherd divideth his sheep from the goats.

And He shall set the sheep on His right hand, but the goats on the left.

Then shall the King say unto them on His right hand, Come, ye blessed of My Father, inherit the kingdom prepared for you from the foundation of the world;

For I was hungry, and ye gave Me food; I was thirsty, and ye gave Me drink; I was a stranger, and ye took Me in;....

Then shall He say also unto them on the left hand, Depart from Me, ye cursed, into everlasting fire, prepared for the devil and his angels;.... *(Matthew 25:31-46)*

JEHOVAH'S WITNESSES on THE LAST THINGS

The BIBLE on THE LAST THINGS

The "sheep," those individuals among the nations who manifested their true faith by showing kindness toward Christ's "brethren" (v. 40), will enter the Millennium.

The "goats," those individual Gentiles who persecuted Christ's brethren, will be sent to hell, which has been "...prepared for the devil and his angels" (v. 41).

All those outside of the New World society will perish along with Satan and his demons. More than two billion will die.
(*You May Survive Armageddon into God's New World*, p. 341)

Thus we see the falsity of the Jehovah's Witness claim that only those "of the New World Society" (Jehovah's Witnesses) will survive Armageddon.

Their "2 billion will die" figure is man-made and again unbiblical—a guess which may or may not prove to be close.

During the 1000 year reign the 144,000 will reign and rule with Christ from heaven.
(*From Paradise Lost to Paradise Regained*, p. 211)

Two resurrections during the Millennium:

The Resurrection of Life
The faithful men of God who lived before Pentecost and of other sheep who died before Armageddon.
(*Paradise Lost*, p. 228)

The Resurrection of Judgment
The rest of mankind who have not been judged worthy of being destroyed.
(*Paradise Lost*, p. 229)
These are people whose hearts may have been wanting to do right, but who died without ever having had an opportunity to hear of God's purposes or to learn what he expects of men.
(*Paradise Lost*, p. 229)

And I saw thrones, and they sat upon them, and judgment was given unto them; and I saw the souls of them that were beheaded for the witness of Jesus, and for the word of God, and who had not worshiped the beast [Antichrist], neither his image, neither had received his mark upon their foreheads, or in their hands; and they lived and reigned with Christ a thousand years. *(Revelation 20:4)*

Jehovah's Witnesses tell us that only they will survive Armageddon and only they will rule with Christ in the Millennium.

Revelation 20:4 (quoted above) expressly declares that the martyrs for Christ will rule and reign with Him during the Millennium. These martyrs appear to be representative of all those who have died in Christ. That they are exclusively Jehovah's Witnesses is a man-made, biblically unsupported Jehovah's Witness boast.

JEHOVAH'S WITNESSES on THE LAST THINGS

THE FINAL STATE

The doctrine of a burning hell where the wicked are tortured eternally after death cannot be true, mainly for four reasons: (1) It is wholly unscriptural; (2) it is unreasonable; (3) it is contrary to God's love, and (4) it is repugnant to justice.
(*Let God Be True*, p. 99)

If hell is a place of eternal torment, and the Devil is the chief fireman, who is going to keep up the fire when the Devil is destroyed?
(*Where Are the Dead?*, p. 19)

But are not Satan, the Devil, and his demons down in hell keeping the fires and making it hard for those who are in it? This is what is taught by Christendom's clergy, but you will be surprised to know the Devil never was in such a place.
(*Let God Be True*, p. 93)

Gehenna is for Jehovah's Witnesses a symbol of annihilation—an annihilation from which there is no awakening, and no resurrection.
(*Let God Be True*, p. 96)

The BIBLE on THE LAST THINGS

THE FINAL STATE

But I say unto you that whosoever is angry with his brother without a cause shall be in danger of judgment; and whosoever shall say to his brother, Raca, shall be in danger of the council; but whosoever shall say, Thou fool, shall be in danger of hell fire. (Raca—*"empty headed"—an abusive epithet)*

(Matthew 5:22)

And if thy right eye offend thee, pluck it out, and cast it from thee; for it is profitable for thee that one of thy members should perish, and not that thy whole body should be cast into hell.

And if thy right hand offend thee, cut it off, and cast if from thee; for it is profitable for thee that one of thy members should perish, and not that thy whole body should be cast into hell.

(Matthew 5:29-30)

And it came to pass that the beggar died, and was carried by the angels into Abraham's bosom; the rich man also died, and was buried.

And in hades he lifted up his eyes, being in torments, and seeth Abraham afar off, and Lazarus in his bosom.

And he cried and said, Father Abraham, have mercy on me, and send Lazarus, that he may dip the tip of his finger in water, and cool my tongue; for I am tormented in this flame. *(Luke 16:22-24)*

JEHOVAH'S WITNESSES on THE LAST THINGS
(continued)

People who are cast into Gehenna do not remain in the memory of God. Gehenna, "the second death," and "the lake that burneth with fire and brimstone" all stand for the same thing: total annihilation.
(*The Truth Shall Make You Free*, p. 364)

Such total annihilation is therefore the doom of (1) the "goats" at the Battle of Armageddon, (2) all those who will not be raised during the Millennium, (3) and all those who, though living on the new earth during the Millennium, refuse to obey God's kingdom, (4) and all who follow Satan in his final battle.
(*Let God Be True*, p. 97, 270)

The BIBLE on THE LAST THINGS
(continued)

And whosoever shall offend one of these little ones that believe in Me, it is better for him that a millstone were hung about his neck, and he were cast into the sea.

And if thy hand offend thee, cut it off; it is better for thee to enter into life maimed than, having two hands, to go into hell, into the fire that never shall be quenched.

Where their worm dieth not, and the fire is not quenched.

And if thy foot offend thee, cut it off; it is better for thee to enter lame into life than, having two feet, to be cast into hell, into the fire that never shall be quenched,

Where their worm dieth not, and the fire is not quenched.

And if thine eye offend thee, pluck it out; it is better for thee to enter the kingdom of God with one eye than, having two eyes, to be cast into hell fire,

Where their worm dieth not, and the fire is not quenched. *(Mark 9:42-48)*

And the devil that deceived them was cast into the lake of fire and brimstone, where the beast and the false prophet are, and shall be tormented day and night forever and ever. *(Revelation 20:10)*

And death and hades were cast into the lake of fire. This is the second death.

And whosoever was not found written in the book of life was cast into the lake of fire. *(Revelation 20:14-15)*

THE BIBLE on
THE LAST THINGS
(continued

The Scriptures just quoted amply show and Jesus Christ Himself teaches us that hell (*hades* in the Greek, the "unseen" world of the unsaved dead) is a place of fire and eternal torment.

Its final fruition is a place called, "The Lake of Fire which burneth forever and ever." "Fire" and "forever" are Biblical—even though we admittedly do not know the full chemistry of this fire.

"Annihilation" does not match Christ's words, "...where their worm dieth not...." Anyone who reads Mark 9:42-48 should see that we must choose between Christ's solemn testimony and the human, uninspired theories of the Jehovah's Witnesses.

Typical Kingdom Hall. In 3 years 1969-1971, a total of 434,906 persons joined Jehovah's Witnesses.

JEHOVAH'S WITNESSES On ISRAEL and PALESTINE

To the Jehovah's Witness the recent gathering of the Jews to Palestine is not the beginning of the fulfillment of God's prophecies concerning end-time Israel.

Israel, they claim, will not be the benefactor of the promises of God. According to Jehovah's Witnesses, Israel has been set aside. The promises of God to the Jews are being realized in spiritual Israel, the Jehovah's Witnesses.[20]

THE BIBLE on ISRAEL and PALESTINE

Despite Jehovah Witness claims to the contrary, God's Word clearly declares that the Lord will yet rescue, convert, and restore Israel according to God's ancient promise to Abraham.

Neither shall thy name any more be called Abram, but thy name shall be Abraham; for a father of many nations have I made thee.

And I will establish My covenant between Me and thee and thy seed after thee in their generations for an everlasting convenant, to be a God unto thee, and to thy seed after thee.

And I will give unto thee, and to thy seed after thee, the land wherein thou art a sojourner, all the land of Canaan, for an everlasting possession; and I will be their God. (Genesis 17:5,7,8)

In that day there shall be a fountain opened to the house of David and to the inhabitors of Jerusalem for sin and uncleanness.

And it shall come to pass, in that day, that I will seek to destroy all the nations that come against Jerusalem.

And I will pour upon the house of David, and upon the inhabitants of Jerusalem, the Spirit of grace and of supplications; and they shall look upon Me whom they have pierced, and they shall mourn for Him, as one mourneth for his only son, and shall be in bitterness for Him, as one that is in bitterness for his firstborn.

(Zechariah 12:9-10; 13:1)

---

[20]*Let God Be True*, p. 218.

JEHOVAH WITNESSES on OTHER SUBJECTS

Many of the major doctrines of Jehovah's Witnesses are based on DENIALS.

They deny or refuse to recognize:

1. The Trinity
2. The Deity of Christ
3. The inherent immortality of the soul
4. The total depravity of man
5. The bodily resurrection of Christ
6. The atonement
7. The need of new birth for all
8. The Second Coming of Christ
9. Eternal punishment
10. The promises of God to the nation Israel

THE BIBLE on ISRAEL and PALESTINE
(continued)

Yea, many peoples and strong nations shall come to seek the Lord of hosts in Jerusalem, and to pray before the Lord.

Thus saith the Lord of hosts: In those days it shall come to pass that ten men shall take hold out of all languages of the nations, even shall take hold of the skirt of him that is a Jew, saying, We will go with you; for we have heard that God is with you.

(Zechariah 8:22-23)

Therefore, behold the days come, saith the Lord, that they shall no more say, The Lord liveth, who brought up the children of Israel out of the land of Egypt,

But, The Lord liveth, who brought up and who led the seed of the house of Israel out of the north country, and from all countries to which I had driven them, and they shall dwell in their own land.

(Jeremiah 23:7-8)

There are four buildings in the Watchtower printing plant in Brooklyn. They are connected by ramps as shown in the photograph above. Their bindery has the capacity to bind 50,000 books a **day**. *If the year's production of their Watchtower and Awake magazines alone were placed end to end, they would reach over 25,000 miles!*